Creative Graduate Pathways Within and Beyond the Creative Industries

I0896322

Examining pathways from creative education to work, and preparation for these pathways within higher education programs in the light of long standing labour debates, this book explores the creative launch experiences, destinations, and contributions of graduates emerging into an enormously diverse and heterogeneous creative workforce. Coming from university degree programs that tend to focus on the development of specialist creative disciplinary skills, graduates often emerge into the diverse workforce with fairly narrow career identities. With contributions ranging from quantitative analyses of large longitudinal data sets to in-depth qualitative cases, this book aims to provide a range of studies that speak to the complexity found in creative careers.

This book was originally published as a special issue of the *Journal of Education and Work*.

Ruth Bridgstock is an educational futurist, researcher and scholar of graduate capabilities and learning for the 21st century. She is an Associate Professor at Queensland University of Technology, Australia, she convenes the flagship interdisciplinary Bachelor of Creative Industries course. She is Australian National Senior Teaching Fellow for 'Graduate Employability 2.0', which explores the roles that social networks play in graduate career development.

Ben Goldsmith is Senior Lecturer in Screen and Media, and Program Coordinator of the Bachelor of Creative Industries at the University of the Sunshine Coast, Queensland, Australia. His research interests include media education and the use of screen media in education, Australian cinema, media policy, public service broadcasting, sports media, and smartphone apps.

Jess Rodgers is a sessional academic and Senior Research Assistant for the School of Justice, Queensland University of Technology, Australia. With a background in media, communication and journalism, Rodgers is published in queer theory and queer history, and is a co-editor of *Creative Work Beyond the Creative Industries: Innovation, Employment and Education* (2014).

Greg Hearn is Research Professor in the Creative Industries Faculty at Queensland University of Technology, Australia. His work focuses on policy development and R&D for new technologies and services in the creative industries. His books include *The Knowledge Economy Handbook* (2005 and 2012), and *Eat Cook Grow: Mixing Human-Computer Interactions with Human-Food Interactions* (2013).

Creative Graduate Pathways Within and Beyond the Creative Industries

Edited by

Ruth Bridgstock, Ben Goldsmith, Jess Rodgers and Greg Hearn

Routledge
Taylor & Francis Group
LONDON AND NEW YORK

First published 2017 by Routledge

2 Park Square, Milton Park, Abingdon, Oxfordshire OX14 4RN
52 Vanderbilt Avenue, New York, NY 10017

Routledge is an imprint of the Taylor & Francis Group, an informa business

First issued in paperback 2018

British Library Cataloguing in Publication Data
A catalogue record for this book is available from the British Library

ISBN 13: 978-1-138-23063-7 (hbk)
ISBN 13: 978-0-367-07575-0 (pbk)

Typeset in Times New Roman
by RefineCatch Limited, Bungay, Suffolk

Publisher's Note
The publisher accepts responsibility for any inconsistencies that may have arisen during the conversion of this book from journal articles to book chapters, namely the possible inclusion of journal terminology.

Contents

Citation Information

The chapters in this book were originally published in the *Journal of Education and Work*, volume 28, issue 4 (August 2015). When citing this material, please use the original page numbering for each article, as follows:

Introduction
Creative graduate pathways within and beyond the creative industries
Ruth Bridgstock, Ben Goldsmith, Jess Rodgers and Greg Hearn
Journal of Education and Work, volume 28, issue 4 (August 2015), pp. 333–345

Chapter 1
Digital technology and creative arts career patterns in the UK creative economy
Roberta Comunian, Alessandra Faggian and Sarah Jewell
Journal of Education and Work, volume 28, issue 4 (August 2015), pp. 346–368

Chapter 2
Embedded creative workers and creative work in education
Ben Goldsmith and Ruth Bridgstock
Journal of Education and Work, volume 28, issue 4 (August 2015), pp. 369–387

Chapter 3
Creative work careers: pathways and portfolios for the creative economy
Daniel Ashton
Journal of Education and Work, volume 28, issue 4 (August 2015), pp. 388–406

Chapter 4
The careers of fine artists and the embedded creative
Charlotte Carey
Journal of Education and Work, volume 28, issue 4 (August 2015), pp. 407–421

Chapter 5
The rise of the embedded designer in the creative industries
Katja Fleischmann and Ryan Daniel
Journal of Education and Work, volume 28, issue 4 (August 2015), pp. 422–442

For any permission-related enquiries please visit:
http://www.tandfonline.com/page/help/permissions

Notes on Contributors

Daniel Ashton is a Senior Lecturer at Bath Spa University, UK. His research focuses on working in the cultural and creative industries, and his work has been published in journals such as *Convergence*, *Journal of Cultural Economy*, *Journal of Education and Work*, and the *European Journal of Cultural Studies*. He is the co-editor of *Cultural Work and Higher Education* (2013, with Caitriona Noonan).

Ruth Bridgstock is an educational futurist, researcher and scholar of graduate capabilities and learning for the 21st century. An Associate Professor at Queensland University of Technology, Australia, she convenes the flagship interdisciplinary Bachelor of Creative Industries course. She is Australian National Senior Teaching Fellow for 'Graduate Employability 2.0', which explores the roles that social networks play in graduate career development.

Charlotte Carey is Senior Lecturer in Creative Industries Marketing at the Birmingham City Business School, UK. Her research focuses on the creative sector and entrepreneurship education. She is co-chair of the 'Creative Industries Entrepreneurship' track for the Institute of Small Business and Entrepreneurship conference, and her PhD is currently being developed for publication.

Roberta Comunian is a Lecturer in Creative and Cultural Industries in the Department of Culture, Media and Creative Industries at King's College London, UK. Her work focuses on the relationship between arts, cultural regeneration projects, and the cultural and creative industries, she has published extensively on the career opportunities and patterns of creative graduates in the UK.

Ryan Daniel is a Senior Researcher in Creative Arts and Creative Industries at James Cook University, Australia. His research has been published in *Arts and Humanities in Higher Education*, *CoDesign*, *Music Education Research*, and the *British Journal of Music Education*.

Alessandra Faggian is an Associate Professor in the Economics Department at Ohio State University, Columbus, OH, USA, and co-editor of *Papers in Regional Science*. Her research explores regional and urban economics, demography, labour economics, and the economics of education. Her publications have covered migration, human capital, labour markets, creativity, and local innovation and growth.

Katja Fleischmann is a design educator and researcher with extensive knowledge of global and national issues driving the design profession. Her research interests span a variety of areas, including future models of design education, design thinking as a tool for social change, creativity and innovation, and multi- and trans-disciplinary design processes.

Ben Goldsmith is Senior Lecturer in Screen and Media, and Program Coordinator of the Bachelor of Creative Industries at the University of the Sunshine Coast, Queensland, Australia. His research interests include media education and the use of screen media in education, Australian cinema, media policy, public service broadcasting, sports media, and smartphone apps.

Greg Hearn is Research Professor in the Creative Industries Faculty at Queensland University of Technology, Australia. His work focuses on policy development and R&D for new technologies and services in the creative industries. His books include *The Knowledge Economy Handbook* (2005 and 2012), and *Eat Cook Grow: Mixing Human-Computer Interactions with Human-Food Interactions* (2013).

Sarah Jewell is a Lecturer in Economics at the University of Reading, UK. Her research interests lie in the fields of labour economics, the economics of higher education, and life satisfaction. She has published in journals including the *Oxford Economic Papers*, *Regional Studies*, *Feminist Economics*, and the *International Review of Finance*.

Jess Rodgers is a sessional academic and Senior Research Assistant for the School of Justice, Queensland University of Technology, Australia. With a background in media, communication and journalism, Rodgers is published in queer theory and queer history, and is a co-editor of *Creative Work Beyond the Creative Industries: Innovation, Employment and Education* (2014).

INTRODUCTION

Creative graduate pathways within and beyond the creative industries

Ruth Bridgstock, Ben Goldsmith, Jess Rodgers and Greg Hearn

Australian Research Council Centre for Creative Industries and Innovation, Queensland University of Technology, Brisbane, Australia

This special issue explores the nuances of graduate creative work, the kinds of value that creative graduates add through work of various types, graduate employability issues for creative graduates, emerging and developing creative career identities and the implications for educators who are tasked with developing a capable creative workforce. Extant literature tends to characterise creative careers as either 'precarious' and insecure, or as the engine room of the creative economy. However, in actuality, the creative workforce is far more heterogeneous than either of these positions suggest, and creative careers are far more complex and diverse than previously thought. The task of creative educators is also much more challenging than previously supposed. In this introductory article, we commence by providing a brief overview of the creative labour debates, and the evidence for each position. We present the latest literature in this area that starts to speak to how diverse and complex the landscape of creative work actually is. We then introduce each of the articles in this special issue and indicate how they contribute to a more multi-faceted picture of creative activity, and the lives and career trajectories of graduates from creative degrees.

Scholarly discussions of the creative workforce invariably take one of two seemingly incompatible positions. First, cultural studies scholars have spent considerable time describing the ongoing employment insecurity of those involved in creative work, and the antecedents and effects of this employment 'precarity'. In striking contrast to this position is a significant body of policy and large scale empirical work that demonstrates the importance of creative work and workers to the innovation economy and economic growth. These two positions are typically presented as incompatible with one another, and remarkably few attempts have been made to achieve any kind of rapprochement between the two. However, recent investigations propose that the creative workforce is much more heterogeneous than either of these positions suggest; that creative workers are found throughout the economy and not just within the creative and cultural sectors; that certain creative activities, industry segments and sectors are associated with greater precarity and/or greater economic growth than others; that, therefore, creative careers are far more complex and diverse than previously thought; and following on from all of this that the task of creative educators is much more challenging than previously supposed.

This special issue explores the nuances of creative work, the kinds of value that creative workers add through work of various types, creative career identities and the implications for educators who are tasked with developing a capable creative workforce. In this introductory article, we commence by providing a brief overview of the creative labour debates, and the evidence for each position. We present the latest literature in this area that starts to speak to how diverse and complex the landscape of creative work actually is. We then introduce each of the articles in the special issue and indicate how they contribute to a more multi-faceted picture of creative activity.

Precarious creative work

Creative careers have traditionally been described as 'precarious' – that is, involving chronic unemployment and underemployment. Characterisations of 'portfolio careers' comprising piecemeal creative and non-creative jobs, short-term project-based and self-employment-based work abound (see for example, Bridgstock 2005; Ross 2009; Throsby and Zednik 2010). Some theorists (see for example Hall 1996; Howkins 2001) have touted lifestyle benefits of the varied, entrepreneurial aspects of the portfolio career, including flexibility, autonomy and excitement. Recently Morgan, Wood, and Nelligan (2013) suggested that many young creative workers have started to internalise these values, finding portfolio work both liberating and adaptive – a phenomenon Neff (2012) terms 'venture labour'.

However, a significant number of studies indicate that creative workers are often driven to portfolio working arrangements through financial necessity or industry norms and configurations (in the creative industries, much work is project-based and, therefore, of finite length). In portfolio work, the worker assumes individual risk and responsibility for all aspects of career, including those due to economic fluctuations, market and supply chain vagaries, and personal misfortune (Gregg 2011; Neff 2012).

Cultural economists, such as Menger (1999), indicate that an oversupply of creative workers is part of what underlies the precarity phenomenon. According to this school of thought, creative workers derive 'psychic income' from creative work and are, therefore, likely to remain in the industry despite inadequate financial income, underemployment and other adversity. The possibility of a lucky break leading to exceptional success can also be a significant factor (Taylor and Littleton 2008). Rather than going in search of better employment prospects in other industries, creative workers will often remain and 'self-exploit', by working free or at reduced rates (Hesmondhalgh and Baker 2010).

Precarity and self-exploitation both appear to be very common among graduates of creative degrees as they move into the world of work. Creative graduates can struggle through an extended education to work transition involving episodes of unpaid work experience and internships, additional education or training, and reliance on family, social security and/or 'day jobs' for financial support (Galloway et al. 2002). Studies of graduate transitions indicate that many students also experience a significant period of personal and professional identity uncertainty (Buckham 1998; Nystrom 2009). Further, the social network-based informal processes involved in finding or creating creative work can be a significant barrier to entry (McRobbie 2002). Some scholars have argued that these 'who you know' job acquisition and creation processes are a mechanism for exclusion and discrimination (Lee 2011).

The creative economy

Over the last 15 years, a body of literature in striking contrast to the 'precarious labour' literature has arisen. This 'creative economy' corpus argues that creative work and creative workers are of vital importance to economic growth in post-industrial economies, via the addition of creative and cultural value to national innovation systems (Hearn and Bridgstock 2010; Cunningham 2014b). This work draws upon earlier commentary around the 'culturalisation' of industry (Lash and Urry 1994). Creative economy theorists argue that creative and cultural knowledge and skills, along with digital capability, drive innovation throughout the economy, reaching beyond the creative industries (Potts and Cunningham 2008; Hearn et al. 2014). According to Bakhshi, Freeman, and Higgs (2012, 45), 'the creative industries bring together a particular combination of [creative] content and ICT skills; their integrity as an emerging economic entity relies on this combination'. These theorists argue demand for creative workers is in fact increasing and that these workers enjoy conditions comparable to the rest of the workforce (see for example, Cunningham 2014a).

In making these claims, creative economy scholars have relied on evidence from large scale statistical industry mapping studies, beginning with the Creative Industries Mapping Study by the UK Department for Culture, Media and Sport (DCMS 1998) and continuing using various methodologies and in various countries. These scholars consistently report higher-than-average growth of the size of the creative industries as an industry sector and in the size of the creative workforce. The next section of this article presents an overview of one dominant creative workforce mapping methodology: The Creative Trident.

The Creative Trident: within and beyond the creative industries

Over the last decade, the Australian Research Council Centre of Excellence for Creative Industries and Innovation (CCI) has been engaged in measuring the creative workforce using a methodology that relies on census data (see Cunningham 2014a for a description of the development). The 'Creative Trident' was thus developed out of an observation that the size and significance of the creative industries cannot be measured accurately by examining industry activity in isolation. CCI researchers suggest that previous mapping studies have underestimated the creative workforce by up to 40% (Cunningham 2014a).

The Creative Trident model incorporates: (1) the total of creative occupations within the core creative industries (specialists); (2) the creative occupations employed in other industries (embedded); and (3) the business and support occupations employed in creative industries, which are often responsible for managing, accounting for and technically supporting creative activity (support). According to the Trident model, the number of people employed in the 'creative economy' is the total of creative industries employment plus embedded employment. In this model, creative industries and occupations comprise architecture, design and visual arts; music and the performing arts; film, radio and television; writing and publishing; advertising and marketing, and software and digital content (Table 1).

Creative Trident mapping reveals that in a number of economies, the creative workforce is growing at a faster rate than the general economy and that on average; the creative workforce earns salaries above national averages. The Trident has also demonstrated that more creative workers are employed in other sectors (embedded) than are found as specialists inside the creative industries sectors, thus providing support for the notion that

Table 1. The Creative Trident.

	Employment in creative industries	Employment in other industries	Total
Employment in creative occupations	Specialist creatives	Embedded creatives	Total employment in creative occupations
Employment in other occupations	Support workers		
Total	Total employment in creative industries		Total creative workforce

creative activity is important throughout the economy (Cunningham 2014b). Further, embedded creative workers seem to experience precarious labour conditions to a lesser extent than specialists. When Potts and Shehadeh (2014) analysed the large scale longitudinal survey of Australian Household, Income and Labour Dynamics, they found that embedded creative workers were just as likely as Australian workers in general, to be employed in secure, full-time jobs.

Creative Trident mark II

In 2012, the Creative Trident methodology was further refined to identify two creative activity groups: *cultural production*, comprising the sectors and occupations concerned with the production of cultural artefacts and experiences for final consumption (B2C), including film, television and radio, publishing, music, performing arts and visual arts; and *creative services*, comprising the sectors and occupations primarily concerned with business-to-business activities like design, architecture, software and digital content, advertising and marketing (Cunningham 2014a). This categorisation of creative activity allowed for acknowledgement and exploration of the diversity of economic contribution made by different areas of the creative workforce. Through Creative Trident mark II, it was observed that the majority of above-average growth in the creative workforce was generated within creative services, either in creative service industries (support and specialists) or creative service occupations embedded in other industries (embedded in cultural production industries as well as non-creative industries). The Creative Trident mark II outcomes for Australia 2006–2011 are shown in Table 2.

Table 2 shows that between 2006 and 2011, Australia's creative economy as a whole grew faster than the economy as a whole (2.8% as opposed to 2.0%) and that the majority of growth is found in creative services industries, with large creative services industry growth in cultural production jobs, creative services jobs, support jobs and also growth in creative

Table 2. Creative economy employment growth rates by Trident mark II categories based on 2006 and 2011 Australian Census data.

	Cultural production sectors (%)	Creative services sectors (%)	Other sectors (%)
Cultural production occupations	2.60	3.50	−0.80
Creative services occupations	1.70	4.80	2.50
Support occupations	−0.20	4.30	
	Creative economy 2.8 Rest of economy 2.0		

services jobs embedded in other sectors. For cultural production industries, growth rates above the economy only occurred for cultural production jobs in the core cultural production industries, with negative growth rates recorded for support occupations in cultural production and also cultural production embedded roles.

Relatively high growth patterns in creative services and creative service occupations embedded in other industries would seem to be in line with the progressive embedding of digital applications and services into the general economy, including online and digital communication, design, advertising and software/apps development (see Cunningham 2014b and Goldsmith 2014 for further discussion of this). Within the digital economy, there is large and growing core demand for converged digital technologies of production, reproduction and dissemination, such as digital and social tools and media, and a growing general digital, design and communications skill base and consciousness. On the other hand, cultural production is typified by the 'A list/B list', 'nobody knows' and 'arts for art's sake' dicta proposed by Caves (2000), with demand subject to fluctuation and tied to the availability of discretionary income.

Under Trident mark II analysis, cultural production creative workers and segments are argued to be more likely to be associated with precarious employment. Self-employment statistics can be taken as an indication of this. The 2011 Australian Census analyses reveal that self-employment is far more likely, at 13%, among workers within the creative industries, than the workforce overall, at 6%. Within the creative industries workforce, self-employment is very likely among those in cultural production more than half (56%) of employment in the industry classification for creative artists, musicians, writers and performers was self-employment.

The need to go deeper than the census

While the high level, census-based studies of the creative workforce are valuable in terms of describing the extent and economic contribution of creative activity, they are also limited, particularly in terms of fine grained investigations into the experiences and behaviour of creative individuals and groups. It is not possible to investigate career trajectories, configurations of current employment (such as the portfolio career) or the relationship of education and qualification to career. For instance, census data are not able to give insights relating to the career development of creative practitioners over the lifespan, the development of career identity and the idea of managing career risk at certain times of life by moving outside the creative industries or moving from the creative arts into other areas of the creative industries (Oakley, Sperry, and Pratt 2008). Nor can census data address the idea that creatives can manage precarity by balancing between a range of labour conditions as part of the portfolio career – for example, by engaging in arts practice on a self-employed basis at the same time as holding down creative services work or even a 'day job'.

Census data collections tend to ask only about the respondent's primary job, thus ignoring portfolio career arrangements entirely; they also categorise by occupational and industry codes that are often outdated in the context of the digital economy, too granular, or too broad for the scope of enquiry (see Goldsmith 2014). These large scale studies can also make overly neat distinctions between employment types, and underreport on creative work that is undertaken as a second or third job and/or undertaken as part of self-employment.

Creative graduate career studies

Various kinds of survey work looking at creative graduate trajectories and outcomes have added some important depth and texture to what is known about creative launch experiences and the early creative career. The *Creative Graduates, Creative Futures* study in the United Kingdom (Ball, Polard, and Stanley 2010) involved 3500 art, media, crafts and design graduates up to eight years after course completion, following the seminal *Destinations and Reflections* study (Blackwell and Harvey 1999). Ball, Pollard, and Stanley (2010) found that 78% of the participants in the study were engaged in creative work of some sort, although creative work was defined very flexibly, including a much broader range of so-called creative occupations than generally accepted (including how creative occupations are defined in the Trident method). This study also found precarious employment among the graduates studied, especially in the first year after graduation, with high levels of self-employment (45% of the participants surveyed) and portfolio working (48% had more than one job) graduation.

Second, creative graduate destinations in the United Kingdom have also been explored through analysis of the UK-wide 'Destinations of Leavers from Higher Education' (DLHE) survey matched with student record data, collected as part of the 'Students in Higher Education' survey. Comunian and colleagues (Comunian, Faggian, and Li 2010; Comunian, Faggian, and Jewell 2011) analysed surveys submitted by graduates from advertising, architecture, crafts, design, film and television, fine art, music, performing arts, technology and writing and publishing disciplines. They found a complex picture of destinations that nonetheless broadly supported the findings of Trident mark II in Australia that some creative graduates (particularly those from largely creative services-related degrees, such as architecture, advertising and publishing) were much more likely to be employed full time and with higher wages than others (particularly those from broadly cultural production-related degrees, such as craft, and the fine and performing arts).

In Australia, Bridgstock (2011), Bridgstock and Cunningham (2014) conducted a series of 'bottom-up' studies of creative graduate outcomes. Bridgstock (2011) tracked graduates of creative industries undergraduate degree programmes for one year after course completion. While the focus of this study was to identify capability and attitudinal predictors of career success in the creative career, Bridgstock also found a significant disciplinary difference in earnings-based career success measures, with design and digital graduates earning significantly more overall and from creative work than graduates of visual and performing arts programmes. However, the graduates of visual and performing arts programmes maintained high ratings on subjective (self-defined) career success, reflective of Hesmondhalgh and others' (Banks and Hesmondhalgh 2009) suggestions around 'good work' and important non-economic value associated with creative work.

Cunningham and Bridgstock (2012), Bridgstock and Cunningham (2014) conducted a single-institution study of 400 journalism, media and communications graduates going back to 10 years post-course completion. The data in that study supported Creative Trident findings that journalism, media and communications professionals are found throughout the economy. Overall, the graduates in this study enjoyed high levels of employment and gave positive accounts of the relevance of their courses to working life, with minimal precarious employment. In general, courses were regarded as successful in delivering the generic capabilities, skills and orientations that facilitated graduate employability, irrespective of eventual employment type. This finding was congruent with previous data suggesting that creative graduates are fairly well equipped in terms of core disciplinary and broad generic employability skills (such as written communication, critical thinking and numeracy) (Haukka et al. 2010), although they may experience skills gaps in specific multiplatform and digital content, intellectual property and commercial areas (Galloway et al. 2002; Haukka 2011).

Higher education and preparation for creative work

To date, the creative labour debate has not placed much emphasis on its implications for higher education degree programmes. The transition from education to work and career for creative graduates can be enormously challenging for many, as discussed above. Matthews (2011) suggests that the process of moving from creative education to work is more like 'translation' than transition, with graduates engaging in a process of recontextualisation and reinterpretation of knowledge, capabilities and practices acquired during degree courses. Further, the transition can involve substantial professional and personal identity revision.

Higher education can do more than it does presently to smooth graduates' transitions into the workforce. Building into creative programmes critical engagement with creative workforce issues, knowledge of a wider range of career destinations, and higher-level management and self-management capabilities will help to sustain graduates when faced with the many challenges in building creative careers (see also Bridgstock and Carr 2013).

Why this special issue?

This special issue examines pathways from creative education to work, and preparation for these pathways within higher education programmes, in the light of the creative labour debates outlined above. In this special issue, we are concerned with the creative launch experiences, destinations and contributions of graduates emerging into an enormously diverse and heterogeneous creative workforce, coming from university degree programmes that tend to be focussed on the development of specialist creative disciplinary skills and fairly narrow career identities (Bridgstock 2013; Bridgstock and Cunningham 2014). The articles in this special issue range from quantitative analyses of large longitudinal data sets to in-depth qualitative cases. Its contribution is to provide a range of studies that speak to the complexity found in the work life of creative careers.

In the first article, 'Digital technology (DT) and creative arts career patterns in the UK creative economy', Roberta Comunian and colleagues revisit their DLHE survey data-based analytical methodology (see also Comunian, Faggian, and Li 2010; Comunian, Faggian, and Jewell 2011) to explore the roles that digital and creative arts capability play in the creative economy, by examining employment patterns and destinations of DT and Creative Arts and Design (CAD) graduates in the United Kingdom. Following on from propositions out of Trident mark II, the article explores how digital and creative graduates (and their skills) are embedded across industries beyond the creative industries, and how they are concentrated within creative sub-sectors. The authors also look at patterns of employment and unemployment, and the levels of financial reward associated with creative and digital graduate careers, thus teasing out issues of skill and economic value.

In 'Embedded creative workers and creative work in education', Goldsmith and Bridgstock undertake a systematic empirical examination of the connection between creative work and workers, and education work and industries. Taking as their point of departure that education tends to be the most common industry sector into which creative workers are 'embedded' outside the creative industries, they surveyed 900 graduates from creative undergraduate degrees in Australia to examine the prevalence and characteristics of education and education-related employment among creative graduates. Goldsmith and Bridgstock found a very wide range of motivations and drivers for creative graduates engaging in education work, but perhaps most interestingly found that for many of the study participants, education work is often imbued with creativity and that this creative activity is linked strongly with career satisfaction no matter what the job title.

The third article, 'Creative work careers: pathways and portfolios for the creative economy', is concerned with the complex pathways into, within/outside and out of creative work. Daniel Ashton examines the balance of creative and non-creative work in the creative career; challenges to obtaining creative employment; and career exit strategies used by creative workers. He then looks at students from creative courses that go into non-creative occupations in other industries, to highlight the challenge students face around industry expectations and competition with other graduates in the transition from higher education to employment. Ashton's article engages critically with and problematises the Trident model of the creative workforce in the light of the temporary and contingent nature of creative employment.

The 'Careers of fine artists and the embedded creative' is a rich qualitative exploration of the careers of a cohort of graduates from Fine Arts degrees in the decade since graduation. Charlotte Carey writes about strong fine art career expectations reinforced by art school pedagogy, and the artist career identities that continued among the participants, along with a continuing 'compulsion to create'. Career choices and trajectories among the group for the most part enabled participants to continue their arts practices or to satisfy their creativity in other ways. In their 'non-creative' work, for instance, participants' creative expertise often manifested in terms of facilitation of others' creativity. While the careers of participants were complex, entrepreneurship continued to feature in terms of continued forays into self-employment, although Carey notes that creative entrepreneurship education was lacking in their initial degree experiences.

In the final article 'The rise of the embedded designer in the creative industries', Katja Fleischmann and Ryan Daniel present a mixed-methods study of visual design student/graduate career aspirations and expectations, and examine the roles of graduate visual designers currently working in embedded jobs. Their study reveals very low awareness and knowledge among students, and perhaps also tertiary educators, of non-specialist design job roles, and points to the need for explicit inclusion of curricula aimed at embedded career and other related options (such as digital marketing) for graduates. This article emphasises the changing composition of creative work, with increased bundling of creative and digital services within creative roles within and outside the creative industries.

References

Bakhshi, H., A. Freeman, and P. Higgs. 2012. *A Dynamic Mapping of the UK's Creative Economy.* London: NESTA.

Ball, L., E. Pollard, and N. Stanley. 2010. *Creative Graduates, Creative Futures.* London: Council for Higher Education in Art and Design.

Banks, M., and D. Hesmondhalgh. 2009. "Looking for Work in Creative Industries Policy." *International Journal of Cultural Policy* 15 (4): 415–430.

Blackwell, A., and L. Harvey. 1999. *Destinations and Reflections: Careers of British Art, Craft and Design Graduates*. Birmingham, AL: CRQ.

Bridgstock, R. 2005. "Australian Artists, Starving and Well-nourished: What Can We Learn from the Prototypical Protean Career?" *Australian Journal of Career Development* 14 (3): 40–47.

Bridgstock, R. 2011. "Skills for Creative Industries Graduate Success." *Education and Training* 53 (1): 9–26.

Bridgstock, R. 2013. "Not a Dirty Word: Arts Entrepreneurship and Higher Education." *Arts and Humanities in Higher Education* 12 (2–3): 122–137.

Bridgstock, R., and L. Carr. 2013. "Creative Entrepreneurship Education for Graduate Employability in the Creative Arts." In *The CALTN Papers: The Refereed Proceedings of the Creative Arts Learning and Teaching Network Symposium 2013*, edited by J. Holmes, 8–35. Hobart: Tasmanian College of the Arts, University of Tasmania and the Creative Arts Learning and Teaching Network.

Bridgstock, R., and S. Cunningham. 2014. "Graduate Careers in Journalism, Media and Communications Within and Outside the Sector: Early Career Outcomes, Trajectories and Capabilities." In *Creative Work Beyond the Creative Industries: Innovation, Employment and Education*, edited by G. Hearn, R. Bridgstock, B. Goldsmith, and J. Rodgers, 226–244. Cheltenham: Edward Elgar.

Buckham, L. 1998. "'Perhaps We're Thinking There Isn't a Career Out There for Us': A Study of Undergraduates' Attitudes to Their Future Prospects." *British Journal of Guidance and Counselling* 26 (3): 417–433.

Caves, R. E. 2000. *Creative Industries: Contracts Between Art and Commerce*. Cambridge: Harvard University Press.

Comunian, R., A. Faggian, and S. Jewell. 2011. "Winning and Losing in the Creative Industries: An Analysis of Creative Graduates' Career Opportunities Across Creative Disciplines." *Cultural Trends* 20 (3–4): 291–308.

Comunian, R., A. Faggian, and Q. C. Li. 2010. "Unrewarded Careers in the Creative Class: The Strange Case of Bohemian Graduates." *Papers in Regional Science* 89 (2): 389–410.

Cunningham, S. 2014a. "Creative Labour and Its Discontents: A Reappraisal." In *Creative Work Beyond the Creative Industries: Innovation, Employment and Education*, edited by G. Hearn, R. Bridgstock, B. Goldsmith, and J. Rodgers, 25–46. Cheltenham: Edward Elgar.

Cunningham, S. 2014b. *Hidden Innovation: Policy, Industry and the Creative Sector*. Lanham, MD: Lexington Books/Rowman and Littlefield.

Cunningham, S., and R. Bridgstock. 2012. "Say Goodbye to the Fries: Graduate Careers in Media, Cultural and Communication Studies." *Media International Australia: Incorporating Culture and Policy* 145: 145–160.

Department for Culture Media and Sport. 1998. *Creative Industries Mapping Document 1998*. London: DCMS.

Galloway, S., R. Lindley, R. Davies, and F. Scheibl. 2002. *A Balancing Act: Artists' Labour Markets and the Tax and Benefit Systems*. London: Arts Council of England.

Goldsmith, B. 2014. "Embedded Digital Creatives." In *Creative Work Beyond the Creative Industries: Innovation, Employment and Education*, edited by G. Hearn, R. Bridgstock, B. Goldsmith, and J. Rodgers, 128–144. Cheltenham: Edward Elgar.

Gregg, M. 2011. *Work's Intimacy*. Cambridge: Polity.

Hall, D. 1996. *The Career is Dead – Long Live the Career: A Relational Approach to Careers*. San Francisco, CA: Jossey-Bass.

Haukka, S. 2011. "Education-to-work Transitions of Aspiring Creatives." *Cultural Trends* 20 (1): 41–64.

Haukka, S., G. N. Hearn, J. Brow, and S. D. Cunningham. 2010. *From Education to Work in Australia's Creative Digital Industries: Comparing the Opinions and Practices of Employers and Aspiring Creatives*. Brisbane: ARC Centre of Excellence for Creative Industries and Innovation.

Hearn, G., and R. Bridgstock. 2010. "Education for the Creative Economy: Innovation, Transdisciplinarity and Networks." In *Education in the Creative Economy*, edited by M. Peters and D. Araya, 93–116. New York: Peter Lang.

Hearn, G., R. Bridgstock, B. Goldsmith, and J. Rodgers, eds. 2014. *Creative Work Beyond the Creative Industries: Innovation, Employment and Education Cheltenham*. London: Edward Elgar.

Hesmondhalgh, D., and S. Baker. 2010. "'A Very Complicated Version of Freedom: Conditions and Experiences of Creative Labour in Three Cultural Industries." *Poetics* 38 (1): 4–20.

Howkins, J. 2001. *The Creative Economy: How People Make Money from Ideas*. London: Penguin.

Lash, S., and J. Urry. 1994. *Economies of Signs and Space*. London: Sage.

Lee, D. 2011. "Networks, Cultural Capital and Creative Labour in the British Independent Television Industry." *Media, Culture and Society* 33 (4): 549–565.

Matthews, N. 2011. "Transition or Translation?: Thinking Through Media and Cultural Studies Students' Experiences After Graduation." *Cultural Studies Review* 17 (2): 28–48.

McRobbie, A. 2002. "Clubs To Companies: Notes on the Decline of Political Culture in Speeded Up Creative Worlds." *Cultural Studies* 16 (4): 516–531.

Menger, P. M. 1999. "Artistic Labor Markets and Careers." *Annual Review of Sociology* 25: 541–574.

Morgan, G., J. Wood, and P. Nelligan. 2013. "Beyond the Vocational Fragments: Creative Work, Precarious Labour and the Idea of 'Flexploitation'." *The Economic and Labour Relations Review* 24 (3): 397–415.

Neff, G. 2012. *Venture Labor: Work and the Burden of Risk in Innovative Industries*. Cambridge, MA: MIT Press.

Nyström, S. 2009. "The Dynamics of Professional Identity Formation: Graduates' Transitions from Higher Education to Working Life." *Vocations and Learning* 2 (1): 1–18.

Oakley, K., B. Sperry, and A. Pratt. 2008. *The Art of Innovation: How Fine Arts Graduates Contribute to Innovation*. London: NESTA.

Potts, J., and S. Cunningham. 2008. "Four Models of the Creative Industries." *International Journal of Cultural Policy* 14 (3): 233–247.

Potts, J., and T. Shehadeh. 2014. "Compensating Differentials in Creative Industries and Occupations: Some Evidence from HILDA." In *Creative Work Beyond the Creative Industries: Innovation, Employment and Education*, edited by G. Hearn, R. Bridgstock, B. Goldsmith, and J. Rodgers, 47–60. Cheltenham: Edward Elgar.

Ross, A. 2009. *Nice Work if You Can Get It: Life and Labor in Precarious Times*. New York: NYU Press.

Taylor, S., and K. Littleton. 2008. "Art work or Money: Conflicts in the Construction of a Creative Identity." *The Sociological Review* 56 (2): 275–292.

Throsby, D., and A. Zednik. 2010. *Do You Really Expect to Get Paid? An Economic Study of Professional Artists in Australia*. Melbourne: Australia Council for the Arts.

Digital technology and creative arts career patterns in the UK creative economy

Roberta Comunian[a], Alessandra Faggian[b] and Sarah Jewell[c]

[a]*Department for Culture, Media and Creative Industries, King's College, London, UK;* [b]*AED Economics Department, The Ohio State University, Columbus OH, USA;* [c]*School of Economics, University of Reading, Reading, UK*

In this article, we ask what role both digital and artistic human capital play in the creative economy by examining employment patterns of digital technology (DT) and creative arts and design (CAD) graduates. Using student micro-data collected by the Higher Education Statistical Agency (HESA) in the United Kingdom, we investigate the characteristics and location determinants of these graduates. The article deals specifically with understanding how digital and creative skills in the UK are embedded across industries, or are concentrated in creative sub-sectors. Furthermore, it explores the role that these graduates play in each of the different sectors and their financial rewards. Findings suggest that digital technology graduates tend to concentrate in the software and gaming sub-sector of the creative industries, but also are likely to be in embedded creative jobs outside of the creative industries. DT and CAD graduates are more likely to be in a creative job than other graduates. Although they are more likely to be in full-time employment than part-time or self-employment, DT graduates suffer from a higher level of unemployment than CAD graduates.

Introduction

A recent report from National Endowment for Science Technology and the Arts (NESTA 2011) highlights the role played by higher education in the creative digital economy and emphasises the important cross-over between artistic skills and STEM skills.[1] However, there is a lack of comparative knowledge regarding what kinds of creative careers are undertaken by creative arts and design (CAD) and digital technology (DT) graduates, including their economic rewards and job patterns. The current article argues that, in order to understand better the roles and importance of digital technologies in the creative economy, we first need a better understanding of the role played by digital technology skills in relation to creative skills, both within and outside the creative industries.

The article aims to address this specific gap, exploring the relationship between creative arts and digital technology skills in the creative economy in the UK. It considers the roles of both DT and CAD graduates in the creative labour market and offers a profile of their occupations, including the industry in which they are employed and their salary. It also studies which factors influence the probability of these graduates finding a creative job (in or outside of the creative industries).

The article is divided into 4 sections. Section 1 introduces the literature and previous research in the field. Section 2 briefly describes the data and methodology used. Section 3 presents the results. Finally, Section 4 discusses the findings, presents a conclusion and further possible future research avenues.

Research landscape: the creative economy and creative and DT skills

The intrinsic use of DT is a key factor driving most of the sectors of contemporary economies, but it is said to play a fundamental role in the creative industries. For example, digital technology plays an ever growing role in the distribution and commercialisation of creative content, within the creative supply chain, and also in the creation of new markets for creative and cultural products (Potts et al. 2008). Moreover, Potts and Cunningham (2008) questioned the narrow perspective of considering the 'creative industries' as a sector of the economy; instead they argue for an 'innovation model' of the creative industries, where creative industries are considered a part of the broader innovation system, contributing to the generation of ideas and technology. In addition, the literature tends to highlight the complex interplay between artistic and DT skills, which need to be present within the creative industries (Healy 2002). However, Skillset (2010, 26) highlights that 'across many sectors of the creative industries, skills in short supply from new entrants relate directly to new and digital technology'. In the creative media industries, the most common areas of training needs identified by employers are related to new and digital technology (one in four people) (Skillset 2009, 19).

The 2011 NESTA report – looking at the video games and visual effects sector – suggests that many of the university courses in those subject areas do not prepare students to be 'industry-ready'. They argue that 'Universities too often appear to be focused on attracting students onto their course rather than pushing up the standards of those graduating' (NESTA 2011, 47). While this highlights the importance of gaining a better understanding of the labour market outcomes of graduates from these disciplines, it does not say much about how their job opportunities compare with other groups and in which sector their best job opportunities lie. It is crucial to understand whether the phenomenon mentioned in the NESTA report is specific to these subjects or is widespread and follows from the relentless expansion in higher education. What value does a 'digital' course provide and how does it compare with other disciplines? Are the much-advertised 'creative' occupations a good fit for graduates in these areas?

These kinds of considerations motivate our focus on creative careers. While it is widely acknowledged in the literature that careers in creative fields tend to be unstructured, often relying on part-time and temporary work as well as on low wages, our knowledge of how these characteristics differ across the creative industries and occupational sectors is very limited. There are many studies looking at the career difficulties faced by artists and creative workers, such as unstable working patterns, over supply and lower economic rewards (see, for example, Menger 1999; Comunian 2009). However, while these studies provide interesting insights on key issues faced by creative workers, they are limited due to their clustering of artistic and new digital professionals into a single group. Other authors have tried to look more closely at the workers in the digital and media industries (see, for example, Pratt 2000; Christopherson 2002). However, most research in this field builds on qualitative analysis and case studies, which does not allow for comparative work across different creative disciplines.

Therefore, we will consider specifically the role of skills and education, using the Higher Education Statistical Agency (HESA) data. The HESA surveys are a very rich source of data and include individual information on all UK students and a large sample of all UK graduates. As such, the HESA data allow for a comparison of how different graduates from different disciplines, institutions and with different final grades fair when entering the labour market, and how well their skills match what the market really requires.

Following these considerations, the article aims to address three core research questions in relation to the role played by DT skills – represented by DT graduates – in the creative economy:

- What role do DT and CAD graduates play in the creative labour market?
- What are the industries entered and jobs undertaken by DT and CAD graduates?
- What factors influence the probability of a DT and CAD graduates entering a creative job (within and outside the creative industries) and what are the determinants of higher salaries in creative jobs?

Data, definitions and methodology

HESA data

Our analysis is based on data from the 'Destinations of Leavers from Higher Education' (DLHE) survey matched with their student record data, collected as part of the 'Students in Higher Education' survey. These data are collected by the UK HESA. The DLHE survey, generally targeted towards British domiciled students, is a survey undertaken every year to collect information about graduates' employment activities six months after graduation. We concentrate our analysis on British domiciled students and, in particular, we focus on the cohort of students who graduated in 2005 (with employment data for 2006). As we are interested in employment patterns, these two years are useful as they capture the pre-recession period.

The DLHE survey includes information on the graduate's employment, in particular: salary level; employer industry code (4-digit SIC code); job occupational code (4-digit SOC code); and location of employment (postcode). From the student record data, we obtain information on personal characteristics (such as gender, age and ethnicity); subject of study (at the 4 digit Joint Academic Coding System (JACS) code); mode (full-time vs. part-time) and level of study (e.g. postgraduate, undergraduate); and degree results and institution attended. Our sample size is the 313,800 graduates who responded to the DLHE survey. This is a response rate of 71% from the sample of all British graduates eligible for a DLHE return. Our sample size reduces slightly to 303,178 when we exclude those who provided an explicit refusal to the DLHE or were undertaking combined subjects (since it was not possible to classify these subjects). Postgraduates consist of 24% of our sample, 66% are undergraduates, and 10% are other undergraduates below first degree level (such as higher national diplomas and certificates, foundation degrees).

While the figures we present for graduates within the creative industries are only a part of the overall creative workforce, there are key supporting factors highlighting the relevance of this data (DaVanzo 1976): the creative industries workforce in the UK is young – 42% in creative media are under 35 years old and 52% in the overall creative and cultural sector are under 40 years; the creative industries workforce in the UK is highly skilled – 57% in creative media and 54% in the creative and cultural sector have a degree or equivalent qualification (compared with only 35% of the general workforce).

Definitions: subjects and creative industries and occupations

In order to fully explore the role played by different skills in the creative job market, we group creative graduates in two main categories: digital technology graduates and creative arts and design graduates, according to their main subject of study (identified by HESA through JACS codes). All the other graduates are included in the group 'other'.

Our subject definition is as follows:

(1) Digital technology (DT), selected codes from G,H,J;[2]
(2) Creative arts and design (CAD), all JACS codes beginning with W;
(3) Other (all other JACS codes)

As in previous investigations (Comunian, Faggian, and Li 2010; Comunian, Faggian, and Jewell 2011), we base the definition of creative occupations on the Department for Culture, Media and Sport (DCMS) definition (2001). Using a creative occupations approach as developed by NESTA (2008), we consider both creative careers within the creative industries but also creative jobs 'embedded' in other sectors. Our definition of a creative job is based on the initial DCMS definition based on 4-digit SIC codes (DCMS 2010). However, we supplement this definition with the inclusion of other creative workers based in sectors outside the creative industries as identified by a more recent DCMS document (DCMS 2010). Moreover, we also took on board some of the criticisms to the DCMS definition provided by a recent report by NESTA (2008). Following NESTA (2008), we also classify a creative job as follows:

- Specialist – in a creative occupation within the creative industries;
- Support – in a non-creative occupation within the creative industries;
- Embedded – in a creative occupation outside the creative industries.

When breaking down creative jobs into finer categories, we use the following groups: advertising, architecture and design engineers, design, designer fashion and crafts, film, TV, radio and photography, music and visual performing arts, publishing, software, computer games and electronic publishing, libraries, museums and cultural activities. These finer categories are important as creative jobs are very heterogeneous, and there are substantial differences between sub-groups (Mcgranahan, Wojan, and Lambert, 2011).

The specific JACS codes corresponding to DT areas of study were chosen to be representative of digital technology graduates because they were identified as having a high concentration of digital technology content (both theory and practice). In particular, the subject groups of G4 Computer Science, G5 Information Science, G6 Software Engineering and G7 Artificial Intelligence were the main disciplinary areas of reference and were included in their entirety. H6 Electronic and Electrical Engineering was also considered an important component but some sub-groups like Bioengineering were excluded. Other smaller code groups were included that were specific to the technological dimension of creative production, for example audio technology and music recording (see Appendix 1 for details).

Methodology

The article employs a three-step methodology. Firstly, we use descriptive statistics to explore the sample, how many graduates enter the labour market and how many specifically enter the creative workforce (either through creative jobs, work in creative industry sectors, or both). We will also consider how many graduates from digital technology and how many from other degrees enter the digital technology sector. Secondly, we present some descriptive statistics focused specifically on the differences across creative industries sub-sectors. We explore which sub-sectors of the creative industries, and also which areas outside the creative industries, employ more digital technology graduates. We ask which types of jobs (specialist; support; embedded) they enter in each industry sector. Further, we will examine which industry sectors offer them better opportunities to undertake graduate-level jobs. Within this analysis, we also consider the reasons that these graduates provided for taking a job in the creative industries.

Lastly, we use a logit model to examine the factors influencing the probability of digital technology graduates entering a creative occupation. Here, we only use first degree students so we can examine the effect of degree class as others have done (Faggian et al. 2012). We also consider the economic rewards for undergraduate students, and what influence this might have on the choice of entering the creative industries. We make use of the salary variable obtained in the DLHE survey (with the full-time equivalent asked for those working less than full-time), which is reported by 67,720 employed first degree individuals, and we exclude those who claim to earn less than the national minimum wage and those who report values of £100,000 above as a result of the possibility of an extra 0 having been accidently added, leaving 59,406 salary observations.[3]

Results

Descriptive statistics

The first part of this section provides some basic statistical information on our sample with a specific focus on creative graduates and their labour market outcomes. As shown in Table 1, the DT (7%) and CAD students (9%) comprise about 16% of our sample student population. Although these might seem small percentages, there has been a growing interest in these subjects, and many institutions have seen a substantial increase in the number of students taking these courses in the last decade (Heartfield 2005). The HESA (2009) highlights the steady growth of creative subject areas. Between 2003/2004 and 2007/2008 architecture, building and

Table 1. Destination by subject group.

	Creative graduates		Other
	DT	CAD	
No of obs.	21,435	27,713	254,030
%	7.07	9.14	83.79
Destination (%)			
Labour market entrants	73.07	73.28	77.68
Full-time paid work	54.82	43.72	57.52
Freelance/self-employed	2.71	8.53	1.48
Part-time paid work	6.78	12.01	7.4
Voluntary/unpaid work	0.52	1.09	0.71
Work and study	8.24	7.92	10.57
Non-labour market entrants	26.93	26.72	22.32
Further study only	13.02	12.43	12.67
Assumed to be unemployed	9.26	8.36	4.55
Not available for employment	3.41	4.09	4.13
Other	1.24	1.83	0.96

planning has shown the highest growth of 34.2%, creative arts and design have shown a 14.2% increase, while mass communication and documentation 7.3%. The overall growth across all subjects has been 4.8%.

Past research has shown that creative graduates in general tend to have worse labour market conditions associated with lower paid and part-time jobs (Mcgranahan, Wojan, and Lambert, 2011). DT students exhibit similar statistical profiles to CAD graduates in many respects (see Table 1), but there are some notable differences. On one side, DT graduates have the highest unemployment rate among all graduates (9.3% compared to 4.55% for graduates from other subjects), even compared with CAD graduates (8.4%). On the other, however, DT students are less likely to work on a part-time basis (6.78) or work in voluntary/unpaid jobs (0.52%) compared to other graduates (7.40 and 0.71%), and especially compared to other CAD graduates (12 and 1.1%). The higher unemployment rate can be explained in different ways. It could be linked to an oversupply of students in these subjects – which would go with how popular these courses were in the last decade together with the aftermath of the dot.com bubble bursts – but also to the graduates not having the appropriate skills required by the market (Haukka 2011). There is a general need for universities to look at what kind of graduates are required from the market in an effort to produce the right type of graduate with the desired skills to meet the demand of employers. This is certainly true in the creative industries, but also elsewhere.[4] Another interesting observation – which could be also linked to the higher level of unemployment of DT graduates – is the level of self-employment/freelancing: only 2.71% of DT graduates are working freelance or being self-employed compared with 8.53% of CAD graduates. While our previous knowledge of creative graduates' career patterns remains relevant, it is clear that DT students' experiences differ from CAD graduates. To understand the underlying reasons for this, it is important to explore these differences further.

Table 2 provides a breakdown of the industry sizes (including those within the creative industries) of those employing graduates (based on the graduates in our sample) and whether they are graduate-level jobs, as defined Elias and Purcell (2004), along with a breakdown of which graduate subject areas they employ. The best providers of jobs are the health and social welfare and education sectors, which together employ around 42% of employed graduates and represent 51% of graduate jobs. The creative industries employ 13% of new graduates in the labour market and constitute 16% of graduate-level jobs for new entrants. Within the creative industries, the biggest provider of jobs is the software, computer games and electronic publishing sector, which employed 2.8% of all graduates entering the labour market in 2006 and 3.7% of graduate-level jobs.

It is noticeable – and relatively good news – that a high proportion of jobs taken by graduates are graduate-level jobs and this is particular true in advertising, architecture and design engineering, and software, computer games and publishing. It is also interesting to look at how different degrees are linked to the creative industries. Overall, 58% of graduates employed in the creative industries are from degrees that are neither creative nor linked to DT (in particular 30% are from humanities) (Comunian, Faggian, and Jewell 2014). However, there are clear differences between the creative sub-sectors. In particular, DT graduates make up 67% of graduates employed in the software sector although their skills seem to be of some value also in the design sector (9.2%) and in the 'film, TV, radio and photography' sector (10.2%). As expected, the design and music sectors mainly employ CAD graduates (70 and 50%, respectively). The rest of the creative sub-sectors employ the majority of their graduates from 'other' degrees (for example 57% in the libraries, museums and art gallery sector are humanities students).

What is worth noticing is that in some sub-sectors of the creative economy the skills sought after by employers are very specific and require a specific degree, while in others the more general (and more transferable) skills are very valuable and – in some cases – more valuable than specific ones, making the market more open to competition from graduates in other disciplines (and institutions). This may have some bearing on the differing labour market outcomes experienced by graduates from different degrees. Furthermore, there has also been a broader policy argument for innovation and new technologies to be embedded across different sectors of the

Table 2. Sector size and graduate-level jobs.

	Sector size: No. of jobs	% New graduates employed in this sector	% Graduate-level jobs across sectors	% Jobs in the sector that are graduate level	Subject distribution employment by sector Creative graduates			
					DT	CAD	Other	Total
Creative industries	30,850	13.23	15.96	87.32	18.43	23.36	58.21	100
Advertising	*4720*	2.02	2.66	94.93	3.56	7.99	88.45	100
Architecture and design	*4380*	*1.88*	*2.48*	*95.43*	*4.09*	*4.00*	*91.92*	100
Design, designer fashion and crafts	*4557*	*1.95*	*2.49*	*91.97*	*9.26*	*70.48*	*20.25*	100
Film, TV, radio and photography	*2745*	*1.18*	*1.19*	*73.28*	*10.20*	*35.59*	*54.21*	100
Music and performing arts	*3507*	*1.50*	*1.70*	*81.75*	*3.82*	*49.87*	*46.31*	100
Publishing	*2518*	*1.08*	*1.18*	*78.98*	*3.53*	*12.11*	*84.35*	100
Software, computer games and electronic publishing	*6519*	*2.80*	*3.67*	*94.94*	*66.85*	*2.53*	*30.62*	100
Libraries, museums and art galleries	*1858*	*0.80*	*0.58*	*53.01*	*2.53*	*12.65*	*84.82*	100
Science, technology and engineering	22,230	9.53	10.03	76.27	13.65	3.38	82.97	100
Health and social welfare	51,775	22.20	27.31	89.06	0.94	1.61	97.44	100
Education	45,981	19.72	23.83	87.48	3.05	8.99	87.96	100
Financial, property and business	33,221	14.24	12.72	64.68	5.58	4.93	89.49	100
Public administration	12,443	5.34	3.92	53.28	5.29	3.73	90.98	100
Other	36,718	15.74	6.23	28.63	6.86	14.35	78.79	100
Total	233,218	100	100	72.41	6.71	8.70	84.59	100

creative and cultural industries (NESTA 2010), which our data seem to contradict. However, it is also true that in the creative industries, which is characterised by small and medium size enterprises, collaboration across sectors might take place and may be more advantageous than embedding creative workers across diverse sectors.

The creative labour market and DT graduates

After understanding the main characteristics and work patterns of CAD and DT graduates, we now turn to their interconnection with the creative industries. Table 3a presents the industry distribution of graduate creative jobs, with a further breakdown of the type of creative degree studied. DT (36.35%) and CAD graduates (35.5%) are more likely to enter the creative industries than other industries, as well as being more likely to enter the creative industries compared to other graduates (9.10%). Even so, only a third of DT and CAD graduates end up in the creative industries, with almost 20% of DT students entering the science, engineering and technology industry. It is worth also noticing the importance of education

Table 3a. Sector distribution and creative job type by subject studied.

	DT	CAD	Other
Industry sector (%)			
Creative industries	36.35	35.50	9.10
Science, technology and engineering	19.40	3.70	9.35
Health and social welfare	3.13	4.11	25.57
Education	8.97	20.37	20.50
Financial, property and business	11.85	8.07	15.07
Public administration	4.21	2.29	5.74
Other	16.10	25.96	14.67
Creative jobs within the creative industries (%)			
Advertising	2.96	5.24	23.28
Architecture and design	3.15	2.43	22.45
Design, designer fashion and crafts	7.43	44.64	5.15
Film, TV, radio and photography	4.93	13.58	8.30
Music and performing arts	2.36	24.31	9.06
Publishing	1.57	4.24	11.84
Software, computer games and electronic publishing	76.77	2.29	11.13
Libraries, museums and art galleries	0.83	3.27	8.79
Proportions of specialist, support and embedded creative jobs			
Specialist	32.83	47.48	32.49
Support	14.04	19.47	29.22
Embedded	53.13	33.05	38.29

for CAD graduates 20% (more than double of the digital technology students 9%). Within the graduates entering creative jobs, DT graduates are the most concentrated with 77% going into the software, electronic games and publishing industries. This seems to point to a very good fit between the topics studied at university and the occupation entered, linked mainly to the high level of specialisation of these graduates, although it should also be mentioned that digital work – for its nature and size – often tends to be outsourced rather than incorporated in the functions of other industries.

In terms of category of job role in the creative trident (i.e. specialist, support or embedded), graduates from different subjects not only enter different sub-sectors inside and outside of the creative industries but also work in different roles. For example, 53% of DT students are embedded, with 33% in specialist roles, while only 14% are in support roles. By contrast, CAD graduates are far more likely to be employed in specialist roles (47%) rather than embedded roles (33%).

This seems to highlight the fact that other industries are able to embed DT graduates, offering them creative occupations even outside creative industries (see Table 3b). It also suggests recognition of the value and skills of DT graduates in the broader economy (e.g. a web designer in a manufacturing industry). The fact that DT graduates are less likely to be in specialist positions seems to highlight a difficulty in entering specialist occupations within creative industries, which is comparable to the position occupied by the general 'others' group. Non-creative graduates, with the exception of those from humanities (Comunian, Faggian, and Jewell 2014), tend to play a bigger support role than creative graduates and are less likely to be in specialist roles.

When asked about the reasons for taking their job, 40.5% of DT graduates stated that the 'job fitted into their career plan'. This compared favourably with CAD graduates (37.7%) but negatively with 'other' graduates (47.8%). However, once restricting the sample only to those employed in the creative industries, DT graduates were the most likely to report a good fit (50.7% compared to 48.8% for creative graduates and 46.2% for other graduates). This seems to suggest that although DT students may find it harder to enter the labour market (see the higher level of unemployment in Table 1), those who find a job are more likely to see a fit with their career plan (possibly preferring to be unemployed than finding a non-suitable job) especially in the case of creative jobs. Across all students, it is noticeable that the proportion reporting that they took the job 'To gain experience in order to get the type of job I really want' (26.2% vs. 18.4%) or 'To broaden my experience/to develop general skills' (34.2% vs. 28%) is much higher among creative jobs than non-creative jobs – suggesting that jobs undertaken by graduates in the creative industries are likely to be a stepping stone to a career graduates really want.

Table 3b. Per cent DT graduates and CAD graduates in embedded occupations: sectors and jobs.

	Sectors													
	Science, technology and engineering		Health and social welfare		Education		Financial, property and business		public admin.		Other		Total	
Job categories	DT	CAD	DT	CAD	DT	CAD	DT	CAD	DT	CAD	DT	CAD	DT	CAD
Advertising	0.57	0.77	0.44	0.95	0.17	0.50	1.15	3.29	0.30	0.50	0.71	2.08	3.35	8.08
Architecture and design	3.38	1.62	0.00	0.00	0.07	0.05	0.17	0.36	0.30	0.45	0.27	0.27	4.19	2.75
Design, designer fashion and crafts	4.83	14.40	0.37	0.95	0.68	3.02	1.12	18.37	0.37	1.40	1.32	26.49	8.69	64.62
Film, TV, radio and photography	0.30	0.41	0.00	0.18	0.20	1.94	0.54	4.92	0.07	0.45	0.17	2.08	1.28	9.97
Music and performing arts	0.20	0.45	0.03	0.72	0.14	2.62	0.41	0.99	0.07	0.95	0.17	1.58	1.01	7.31
Publishing	0.03	0.14	0.07	0.23	0.03	0.41	0.00	0.36	0.03	0.14	0.24	1.04	0.41	2.30
Software, computer games and electronic publishing	37.48	1.81	2.53	0.14	4.73	0.09	20.82	0.27	5.88	0.00	8.89	0.54	80.33	2.84
Libraries, museums and art galleries	0.07	0.18	0.07	0.09	0.37	1.08	0.03	0.18	0.17	0.50	0.03	0.09	0.74	2.12
Total	46.87	19.77	3.51	3.25	6.39	9.70	24.23	28.75	7.20	4.38	11.79	34.16	100	100

Graduates were also asked about the self-reported importance of the qualification and subject studied in their work environment. While both DT and CAD graduates are more likely to report the qualification was an 'advantage' (23% vs. 19% of the rest of graduates), they are less likely than graduates from 'other' degrees to report that the qualification was a formal requirement (around 40% for the DT graduates, 31% for CAD graduates and around 46% for other graduates). While this is maybe to be expected for creative arts jobs, it is somewhat more surprising for DT graduates. However, this could be due mainly to 'bad' job-qualification matches. This hypothesis seems to be confirmed by the fact that, once restricting the sample to creative jobs, DT graduates are the most likely to report that the qualification was a formal requirement or expected (around 54% for DT graduates compared to 38% for CAD graduates and 43% for other graduates).

Another interesting finding is that DT graduates are more likely to report that both their degree subject and level are important for their job. This suggests that in their occupations they make use of both the more specific human capital (degree subject) and the more general (transferable) skills developed at university.

When we look more closely at the embedded DT graduates, we find that less than 50% are employed in the science, technology and engineering, and the rest are spread across the other sectors of the economy with a strong presence in the financial, property and business (24.23%) and also the public administration sector (7.20%). Compare with CAD graduates, DT graduates are more embedded in the public administration sector (7.20% vs. 4.38%) and less present in the education sector (6.39% vs. 9.70%). This seems to suggest that a broad range of non-creative industries are able to embed DT graduates. It seems important to notice that DT graduates are, therefore, able to contribute to the broader economy. However, DT graduates are also less likely to be in specialised positions (a creative job within the creative industries).

Entry salary levels of DT graduates are much higher than other creative graduates and are in line with the general graduate population (Table 4). DT graduates earn significantly more by being in a creative job, which is the

Table 4. Mean salary (£) by subject group (Undergraduates only).

	All	Creative job	Non-creative job
DT	19,387	14,828	18,490
CAD	20,486	15,682	18,014
Other	18,520	14,313	18,548
Total	18,286	18,140	18,313

opposite of other graduates who earn significantly less, with no significant difference for CAD students.[5]

Table 5 shows that there are big differences in salaries across the creative industries. On average, the software sector offers higher earnings. In this respect, DT graduates are better placed to receive higher economic rewards for their skills than creative graduates in general. Across the creative industries, embedded creative graduates earn more than graduates in specialist and support roles.

DT graduates in the creative economy: jobs and salary profile

After analysing the overall dynamics and job patterns of DT graduates, we model the likelihood of getting a creative job – for all students and digital technology graduates separately – using a logit model (Table 6). From the results of the logit model, it clearly emerges that DT and CAD graduates are more likely to be in a creative job than other graduates.

While the type of higher education institution attended (i.e. Russell Group, old university, new university or college) does not have an effect on the likelihood of entering the creative economy, it is important for DT graduates. DT graduates for the self-reported most prestigious HEIs (the so-called Russell Group) are almost 34% more likely to find a job in the creative economy. This means that the best graduates prefer creative occupations probably feeling it is the best fit for them. Creative occupations also seem to attract graduates who are younger and did better in their degree (completing with the top grade, i.e. a 'first').

Table 5. Mean salary by sector and creative sub-sector (Undergraduates only).

Creative industries	Mean salary (£)	Mean salary (£) specialised	Mean salary (£) support	Mean salary (£) embedded
Creative industries	18,141	17,557	17,284	19,032
Advertising	17,806	17,496	18,398	17,824
Architecture and design	19,012	16,985	19,654	20,831
Design, designer fashion and crafts	16,183	15,760	15,796	16,554
Film, TV, radio and photography	15,900	16,122	15,751	15,907
Music and performing arts	16,342	16,959	15,046	17,434
Publishing	16,812	16,357	17,223	16,533
Software, computer games and electronic publishing	21,100	20,723	18,843	22,019
Libraries, museums and art galleries	14,451	14,284	14,164	14,838

Table 6. Odds ratio from a logit of the likelihood of getting a creative job.

	All subjects	Digital technology	Creative arts	Other
Personal characteristics				
Female	0.632***	0.647***	0.627***	0.701***
	[–14.175]	[–7.188]	[–10.736]	[–5.784]
Age on graduation (ref: 21 and under)				
22–24	1.083**	1.159**	1.370***	0.984
	[2.375]	[2.022]	[4.859]	[–0.307]
25+	0.757***	0.937	1.508***	0.815**
	[–4.679]	[–0.690]	[4.652]	[–2.046]
Disabled	1.150***	1.134	1.155***	1.177***
	[4.602]	[1.483]	[2.587]	[2.635]
Ethnicity (ref: white)				
Black	0.852**	0.698***	0.975	0.775*
	[–2.249]	[–3.232]	[–0.200]	[–1.769]
Asian	0.746***	0.671***	1.101	0.998
	[–5.687]	[–5.467]	[0.934]	[–0.024]
Mixed	1.131*	1.215	1.416**	0.837
	[1.650]	[0.969]	[2.304]	[–1.063]
Other	1.18	1.009	1.475*	1.096
	[1.605]	[0.048]	[1.652]	[0.403]
Subject group (ref: other subjects)				
Digital technology	4.906***			
	[29.503]			
Creative arts	5.084***			
	[24.555]			
Degree classification (ref: upper second)				
First	1.312***	1.602***	1.619***	1.434***
	[8.880]	[8.154]	[7.935]	[5.827]
Lower second	0.653***	0.577***	0.636***	0.684***
	[–19.671]	[–9.644]	[–9.732]	[–7.829]
Third/pass	0.490***	0.391***	0.466***	0.580***
	[–15.008]	[–11.206]	[–9.157]	[–5.462]
Other degree class	0.396***	0.483***	1.057	1.859**
	[–7.126]	[–3.957]	[0.210]	[2.252]
Institution type (ref: new university)				
Russell group	1.071	1.336***	0.816*	0.902
	[0.818]	[2.825]	[–1.741]	[–0.826]
Other old	0.985	1.290***	1.055	0.675***
	[–0.207]	[3.247]	[0.454]	[–3.082]

(*Continued*)

Table 6. (*Continued*).

	All subjects	Digital technology	Creative arts	Other
HE/FE colleges	0.933	0.79	1.131	0.704**
	[−0.608]	[−1.336]	[0.876]	[−1.986]
Observations	138,213	10,652	15,014	28,233
Log likelihood	−53,600	−6761	−9664	−14,209
LR Chi^2	3254	748	459	187
pseudo r-squared	0.111	0.0539	0.0317	0.02

Note: Robust t statistics in brackets, standard errors clustered at institution level.
***$p<0.01$; **$p<0.05$; *$p<0.1$.

Although we reported the average entry salaries by subject group in Table 4, we did not comment on the possible factors influencing these salaries. Table 7 reports the results of salary regressions where different salary determinants have been included. We report the results separately for all graduates (columns 1 and 2) and for the ones employed in creative jobs (columns 3 and 4). Models 1 and 3 do not include sector fixed effects, while models 2 and 4 do. Although not reported in the table, control variables for gender, age, ethnicity, disability, job attributes (whether part-time, freelance/self-employed) and region of employment were also included.

As shown in Table 7, there is a premium from having a degree from a Russell Group university (about 7% in general, and between 3 and 4% in the creative industries) and graduating with a good grade (a 'first' is associated with around 5% higher entry salary).

DT graduates employed within the creative industries earn about 10% more than the rest of the graduates, although this premium decreases to about 3% once we control for the different creative sub-sectors. Interesting findings come out in model 4 when considering these sub-sectors. Not all the creative sub-sectors are equally advantageous. The software sector pays, on average, the highest entry salaries (about 10% more than other jobs) followed by architecture. The library and film sectors are associated with salary disadvantages of about 16 and 10%, respectively.

Embedded jobs on average pay more than specialist or support jobs, implying that non-creative sectors are willing to pay for creative skills, more than the creative industries. DT students are most likely to be in embedded jobs (see Table 3a). These findings suggest that DT students are particularly valued within the creative industries but even more so in non-creative sectors, while creative graduates earn the least in both the creative and non-creative sectors.

Although not reported in Table 7, some results on the other control variables are worth mentioning. First, female graduates earn less than males.

Table 7. Salary determinants.

	All jobs		Creative jobs only	
	1	2	3	4
Subject group (ref: other)				
Digital technology	0.033***	−0.007	0.103***	0.029***
	[3.797]	[−0.773]	[9.627]	[2.825]
Creative arts	−0.149***	−0.139***	−0.112***	−0.074***
	[−21.011]	[−19.545]	[−11.571]	[−7.894]
Degree classification (ref: upper second)				
First	0.059***	0.056***	0.053***	0.042***
	[12.179]	[11.735]	[8.200]	[7.511]
Lower second	−0.030***	−0.030***	−0.032***	−0.033***
	[−7.515]	[−7.726]	[−5.333]	[−5.327]
Third/pass	−0.01	−0.01	−0.032*	−0.037**
	[−0.416]	[−0.403]	[−1.768]	[−2.063]
Other degree class	0.240***	0.240***	0.005	−0.007
	[7.901]	[7.883]	[0.198]	[−0.302]
Institution type (ref: new university)				
Russell group	0.077***	0.076***	0.040***	0.033***
	[7.105]	[7.147]	[2.819]	[2.781]
Other old	0.015	0.014	0.028*	0.024*
	[1.403]	[1.369]	[1.865]	[1.961]
HE/FE colleges	−0.015	−0.013	−0.016	0.001
	[−1.235]	[−1.068]	[−1.359]	[0.050]
Creative job type (ref: specialist job)				
Support				0.012
				[1.239]
Embedded				0.059***
				[10.055]
Core creative industries (ref: non-creative job/ advertising)[1]				
Advertising		0.009		
		[1.394]		
Architecture		0.028**		0.066***
		[2.233]		[5.840]
Design		−0.009		−0.048***
		[−1.079]		[−4.942]
Film		−0.109***		−0.106***
		[−8.880]		[−9.224]
Music		−0.082***		−0.080***
		[−4.871]		[−5.751]
Publishing		−0.078***		−0.060***

(*Continued*)

Table 7. (*Continued*).

	All jobs		Creative jobs only	
	1	2	3	4
		[–7.049]		[–5.902]
Software		0.118***		0.107***
		[15.112]		[8.785]
Libraries		−0.164***		−0.166***
		[–9.886]		[–10.036]
Observations	59,315	59,284	9239	9234
pseudo r-squared	0.29	0.299	0.259	0.327

Note: Robust t statistics in brackets, standard errors clustered at institution level.
[1]With the inclusion of creative job type advertising is the reference group.
$^{***}p<0.01$; $^{**}p<0.05$; $^{*}p<0.1$.

This is not surprising, and it is consistent with previous studies (Comunian, Faggian, and Li 2010). What is surprising, however, is that this effect is even stronger within creative jobs. While salaries increase with age – as predicted by human capital models (Becker 1993) – this effect is weaker for creatives.

Discussion and conclusions

The article has tried to garner a better understanding of the role played by DT human capital and skills in and beyond the creative industries, with particular focus on the differences between DT graduates and CAD graduates.

The article has explored the role played by DT and CAD graduates in the creative labour market. Our findings highlight that the creative industries employ a variety of graduates but CAD and DT graduates are the most likely student group to enter a creative job. Different sub-sectors of the creative economy employ different types of graduates with DT graduates being a big constituent of the software sector, but also being employed in other creative jobs outside of the creative industries.

In reference to the industries and jobs entered by DT graduates, the article highlights the degree of specialisation of these students but also the potential lack of digital skills (measured here as number of DT graduates) across the creative industries (if we exclude the software sector). DT graduates are more likely to be embedded in non-creative industries than other subjects, with CAD graduates the most likely to be in specialist roles (creative occupations in creative industries). While previous research has shown the poor monetary rewards and unstable employment patterns of creative graduates, graduates in DT show a different profile. DT graduates earn more than CAD graduates and gain more by being in a creative job than others. Within creative jobs, DT graduates earn the most with CAD graduates earning the least. The software sector is the highest paid industry, on average, with architecture and advertising paying more than non-creative industries. DT graduates are more likely to enter the software sector. While their earnings are better, surprisingly they suffer from higher level of unemployment than CAD graduates – highlighting a potential difficulty in entering the job market, possibly linked to a concentration of jobs in specific sectors (and specific locations). More research needs to be done to fully understand why but the motivations – including a low recognition of formal qualification by employers and shortcoming in meeting the industry needs – presented by Haukka (2011) in relation to the Australian case study might be relevant also for the UK. They play a particularly important role in the creative job markets as DT graduates (36.4%) – followed by CAD graduates (36%) –are more likely to enter the creative industries than other sectors.

DT skills can, therefore, be seen as being more broadly relevant to the wider economy than creative arts skills. We have also highlighted how DT graduates follow specific working paths within the creative economy. Different sub-sectors of the creative economy employ different types of graduates and a clear pattern emerges for DT graduates being a big constituent of the software sector (76.77%) with a very marginal presence across other sectors (such as design and film and TV). In fact, while numerous policy documents suggest the important of the digital dimension to the overall creative industries (DCMS and BIS 2009; NESTA 2010), we found little evidence of these skills being employed across other sectors – apart from design and film and television (OECD 2008b). This might be due to the limited size and resources available to arts and cultural industries (in sectors such as publishing or performing arts) and the patterns of collaborative work – which cannot be captured by our data – might facilitate the exchange/embedding of these skills on a temporary basis (Sturgeon 2003). However, DT students clearly see the creative industries as key sectors for their employment and are more likely (when employed in a creative job) than CAD students (but not other subjects) to state the 'job fitted into their career plan'.

Finally, the article has also considered what factors influence the probability of DT graduates to taking a creative job or working in the creative industries and what factors influence higher economic rewards in the creative industries. Our salary model results suggest that DT graduates earn more than CAD graduates, and earn more by being in a creative job, which is where they naturally find their best fit. Furthermore, they are more likely to be in embedded jobs, which were also emerging as being more lucrative. The results also suggest that – in a world where we are witnessing a 'massification' of higher education – having a degree is a necessary but not sufficient condition to find a good graduate entry job in the labour market. For DT graduates, in particular, the specific higher education institution attended matters. Being from a (self-reported) more prestigious HEI (such as the ones belonging to the Russell Group) increases the chance of DT graduates landing a higher paid job as does having graduated with a top mark (i.e. a 'first'). In other words, 'quality' matters.

The article and discussion has been limited to the UK policy framework. While it is clear that this agenda has acquired recently also a strong EU and international dimension (European Commission 2001; Organisation for Economic Co-operation Development 2008a), it was impossible to make broader considerations on these wider contexts, due to the limitations of our data, which refer only to UK graduates. However, the findings from the article are an initial framework for discussion, which could benefit also the international policy arena.

The article has strong policy implications. It seems to suggest that – contrary to common arguments about the role played by technology and innovation in the creative industries – DT expertise (measured by the employment of DT graduates) remain narrowly concentrate in the software industry. Initiatives, such as the 'The Digital R&D Fund for the Arts'[6] (with funding from NESTA, AHRC [Arts and Humanities Research Council] and Arts Council of England), and other policies bodies (including the new Digital Economy programme launched by Research Councils UK) are focusing on bridging this gap, but more needs to be done for the creative industries to benefit from the advances of DT. Although this was not the focus of the article, similar arguments could be made about the limited presence of CAD graduates in the software and gaming sector, contrary to NESTA (2010) which sees the sector as benefitting from both digital and creative skills. The policy implications of the article also extend to higher education policy. It can be argued that, while public policy has tried to promote a broader understanding of the creative industries and their ecology especially in relation to the role played by technology, graduates skills still are very much structured in silos. The fact that DT graduates have greater career opportunities and salaries that other CAD graduate could be a result also of the silos structure of higher education provision. New curricula innovation might provide a solution to a better integration of graduates and skills across the economy (Cunningham and Bridgstock 2012).

Notes

1. STEM subjects are identified with the sciences, technology, engineering and maths.
2. Codes include all computing sciences codes under G, all codes beginning with H6 (except H673 and codes beginning with H68 and H69) and all codes beginning with J52 and J93. See Appendix 1 for more details about the JACS codes used.
3. If we assume that full-time individual's work a minimum of 30 h for 52 weeks and using the minimum wage as of January 2006, which was £4.25, this equates to £6630 which we rounded down to £6500.

4. Although this is a broader question, which the present article cannot answer, there has been research highlighting the need for universities to link more with the creative industries to respond to the needs of employers see Heartfield (2005).
5. *T*-values from significance tests of differences between non-creative and creative job salaries by subject group were –8.1994, –0.2061 and 15.427 for DT, CAD and other graduates respectively.
6. 'The Fund, a partnership between NESTA, the Arts Council England and the Arts and Humanities Research Council (AHRC), is unique in encouraging collaboration between the arts, digital technology providers and the research community in order to undertake experiments from which the wider arts sector can learn' (Arts Council England 2012).

References

Arts Council England. 2012. Digital R&D Fund for the Arts. [Online]. Accessed October 20. http://www.artsdigitalrnd.org.uk.

Becker, G. S. 1993. *Human Capital: A Theoretical and Empirical Analysis, with Special Reference to Education Chicago*. University of Chicago Press.

Christopherson, S. 2002. "Project Work in Context: Regulatory Change and the New Geography of Media." *Environment & Planning A* 34: 2003–2015.

Comunian, R. 2009. "Questioning Creative Work as Driver of Economic Development: The Case of Newcastle-Gateshead." *Creative Industries Journal* 2 (1): 57–71.

Comunian, R., A. Faggian, and S. Jewell. 2011. "Winning and Losing in the Creative Industries: An Analysis of Creative Graduates' Career Opportunities across Creative Disciplines." *Cultural Trends* 20: 291–308.

Comunian, R., A. Faggian, and S. Jewell. 2014. "Embedding Arts and Humanities in the Creative Economy: The Role of Graduates in the UK." *Environment and Planning C: Government and Policy* 32 (3): 426–450.

Comunian, R., A. Faggian, and Li Q. C. 2010. "Unrewarded Careers in the Creative Class: The Strange Case of Bohemian Graduates." *Papers in Regional Science* 89: 389–410.

Cunningham, S. & Bridgstock, R. 2012. Say Goodbye to the Fries: Graduate Careers in Media, Cultural and Communication Studies. *Media International Australia Incorporating Culture and Policy* 145: n.p.

DaVanzo, J. 1976. "Differences between Return and Non-return Migration: An Econometric Analysis." *International Migration Review* 10 (1): 13–27.

DCMS (Department for Culture, Media and Sport). 2001. *Creative Industries Mapping Document*. London: DCMS.

Department for Culture, Media and Sport. 2010. *Creative Industries Economic Estimates*. London: DCMS.

Department of Culture, Media and Sport and Department for Business, Innovation and Skills. 2009. *Digital Britain: Final Report*. London: Department for Culture, Media and Sport and Department for Business, Innovation and Skills.

Elias, P., and K. Purcell. 2004. "Is Mass Higher Education Working? Evidence from the Labour Market Experiences of Recent Graduates." *National Institute Economic Review* 190: 60–74.

European Commission. 2001. *Exploitation and Development of the Job Potential in the Cultural Sector in the Age of Digitalisation*. Brussels: DG Employment and Social Affairs.

Faggian, A., R. Comunian, S. Jewell, and U. Kelly. 2012. "Bohemian Graduates in the UK: Disciplines and Location Determinants of Creative Careers." *Regional Studies* 47 (2): 1–18.

Haukka, S. 2011. "Education-to-work Transitions of Aspiring Creatives." *Cultural Trends* 20 (1): 41–64.

Healy, K. 2002. "Survey Article: Digital Technology and Cultural Goods." *Journal of Political Philosophy* 10: 478–500.

Heartfield, J. 2005. *The Creativity Gap*. London: Blueprint, ETP.

HESA (Higher Education Statistical Agency). 2009. Science and Medicine Studies See Five Year Growth. *Press Release 141*. Cheltenham: HESA.

Mcgranahan, D. A., T. R. Wojan, and D. M. Lambert. 2011. "The Rural Growth Trifecta: Outdoor Amenities, Creative Class and Entrepreneurial Context." *Journal of EconomicGeography* 11: 529–557.

Menger, P. M. 1999. "Artistic Labor Markets and Careers." *Annual Review of Sociology* 25: 541–574.

NESTA (National Endowment for Science Technology and the Arts). 2008. *Beyond the Creative Industries: Mapping the Creative Economy in the United Kingdom*. London: NESTA.

NESTA (National Endowment for Science Technology and the Arts). 2010. *Culture of Innovation*. London: NESTA.

NESTA (National Endowment for Science Technology and the Arts). 2011. *Next Gen. Transforming the UK into the World's Leading Talent Hub for TheVideo Games and Visual Effects Industries. A Review by Ian Livingstone and Alex Hope*. London: NESTA.

OECD (Organisation for Economic Co-operation and Development). 2008a. Digital Content in Transition. *OECD Information Technology Outlook 2008*, 237–282. OECD.

OECD (Organisation for Economic Co-operation and Development). 2008b. *Remaking the Movies: Digital Content and the Evolution of the Film and Video Industries.* OECD.

Potts, J. D., and S. D. Cunningham. 2008. "Four Models of the Creative Industries." *International Journal of Cultural Policy* 14 (3): 233–247.

Potts, J., J. Hartley, J. Banks, J. Burgess, R. Cobcroft, S. Cunningham, and L. Montgomery. 2008. "Consumer Co-creation and Situated Creativity." *Industry and Innovation* 15 (5): 459–474.

Pratt, A. C. 2000. "New Media, the New Economy and New Spaces." *Geoforum* 31 (4): 425–436.

Skillset. 2009. *Strategic Skills Assessment for the Creative Media Industry.* London: Skillset.

Skillset. 2010. *Creative Media Workforce Survey.* London: Skillset.

Sturgeon, T. J. 2003. "What Really Goes on in Silicon Valley? Spatial Clustering and Dispersal in Modular Production Networks." *Journal of Economic Geography* 3 (2): 199–225.

Appendix 1

Creative sub-disciplines	JACS codes
Digital technology	G4 Computer Science (includes sub-disciplines such as Computer Architectures & Operating Systems; Networks and Communications; Human-computer Interaction; Multi-media Computing Science, G5 Information science; G6 Software Engineering (includes sub-disciplines such as Software Design and Programming); G7 Artificial Intelligence; G92 Other Computer Science; H6 Electronic and Electrical Engineering (with the exception of H673 Bioengineering, H68 Optoelectronic Engineering and H69 Electronic and Electrical Engineering Not Classified Elsewhere); J52 Printing (includes sub-disciplines like Offset Lithography, Photo-Lithography, Reprographic Techniques, Screen Process Printing); J93 Technology (includes: Audio Technology and Music Recording)
Creative arts and design	W1 Fine Art; W2 Design Studies; W3 Music; W4 Drama; W5 Dance; W6 Cinematics and Photography;W7 Crafts; W8 Imaginative Writing; W9 Others in Creative Arts and Design
Other	All other JACS codes

Embedded creative workers and creative work in education

Ben Goldsmith and Ruth Bridgstock

Creative Industries Faculty, Queensland University of Technology, Brisbane, Australia

This article is concerned with the many connections between creative work and workers, and education work and industries. Employment in the education sector has long been recognised as a significant element in creative workers' portfolio careers. Much has been written, for example, about the positive contribution of 'artists in schools' initiatives. Australian census analyses reveal that education is the most common industry sector into which creative workers are 'embedded', outside of the core creative industries. However, beyond case studies and some survey research into arts instruction and instructors, we know remarkably little about in which education roles and sectors creative workers are embedded, and the types of value that they add in those roles and sectors. This article reviews the extant literature on creative work and workers in education, and presents the findings of a survey of 916 graduates from creative undergraduate degrees in Australia. The findings suggest that education work is very common among creative graduates indeed, while there are a range of motivating factors for education work among creative graduates, on average they are satisfied with their careers, and that creative graduates add significant creative-cultural and creative-generic value add through their work.

Introduction

In this article, we examine the phenomenon of creative work and creative workers in the education sector. The article is divided into two parts. In the first part, we begin by discussing the shortcomings of top-down approaches, such as using census data, to assess either the extent of creative workers' employment in education, or the variety of contributions people with creative qualifications make in the sector. We then move on to discuss a range of research and reports from a variety of countries that bear on the employment of creative workers and graduates of creative degree programmes in the education sector. Often indirectly, these reports indicate the significance of employment in the education sector for creative workers, frequently as a component of a portfolio career. They also highlight – again, often indirectly – some of the difficulties that arise in attempting either to accurately enumerate the size of the creative workforce in education, or to evaluate the contributions that creative workers or workers with creative training make to the education sector. We conclude this part of the article with a brief discussion of two large surveys of arts and creative graduates, one from the UK and the other from the US, focusing on their findings on embedded creative work in education.

The second part of this article reports some of the findings of a major recent survey of employment and career outcomes for graduates of creative degree programmes from 10 Australian universities. The survey mined a rich lode of information about graduate outcomes from the sample in general. In this article we focus on the findings relating to graduate employment in education occupations and industries. As discussed below, the survey covered a proportion of the degree programmes that broadly correspond with the definition of creative industries and creative occupations used by the Australian Research Council Centre of Excellence for Creative Industries and Innovation (CCI). The survey questioned 916 graduates with conferral dates from 2007 to 2012 in undergraduate degree programmes in visual arts, literary arts/creative writing, performing arts/dance/drama/technical production, music, film, television, new media and animation, or in a more general creative degree programme including a first major in one of the above, about their career trajectories, employment experiences and work histories to five years of post-course completion. The survey produced findings that are somewhat at odds with the findings from analysis of census data, and provided insights that census analysis could not. In the conclusion to this article, we discuss some of the possible reasons for the discrepancies between the data sets, and assess the importance of the new insights into thinking about creative employment in education.

Placing creative work in education in context

Just as careers in the education sector include but are by no means limited to in-class teaching, embedded creative employment, creative work and the work of graduates with creative qualifications in education also extend beyond the classroom. Table 1 lists the Australian and New Zealand Standard Classification of Occupations (ANZSCO) range of educational occupations, while Table 2 lists the occupations reported by respondents to the Australian graduate survey discussed in the second part of this article. And just as there are differences between the various education career roles – for example, between a generalist primary school teacher who teaches art as one among many subjects, a specialist art teacher, an artist-in-residence who may work in

Table 1. Education ANZSCO/ANZSIC codes and corresponding job/industry titles.

ANZSCO code	*Job title*
134111	Child Care Centre Manager
134311	School Principal
134411	Faculty Head
134412	Regional Education Manager
134499	Education Managers nec
241111	Early Childhood (Pre-primary School) Teacher
241112	Kaiako Kohanga Reo (Maori Language Nest Teacher)
241211	Kaiako Kura Kaupapa Maori (Maori-medium Primary School Teacher)
241212	Pouako Kura Kaupapa Maori (Maori-medium Primary School Senior Teacher)
241213	Primary School Teacher
241311	Middle School Teacher (Aus)/Intermediate School Teacher (NZ)
241411	Secondary School Teacher
241511	Special Needs Teacher
241512	Teacher of the Hearing Impaired
241513	Teacher of the Sight Impaired
241599	Special Education Teachers nec
242111	University Lecturer
242112	University Tutor
242211	Vocational Education Teacher (Aus)/Polytechnic Teacher (NZ)
249111	Education Adviser
249112	Education Reviewer
249211	Art Teacher (Private Tuition)
249212	Dance Teacher (Private Tuition)
249213	Drama Teacher (Private Tuition)
249214	Music Teacher (Private Tuition)
249299	Private Tutors and Teachers nec
249311	Teacher of English to Speakers of Other Languages
ANZSIC code	*Industry title*
8410	Preschool Education
8421	Primary Education
8422	Secondary Education
8423	Combined Primary and Secondary Education
8424	Special School Education
8431	Higher Education
8432	Technical and Further Education
8440	Other Education

a school for a short period, an arts academic in an education faculty who works with trainee teachers, and a school administrator or head of department with a background in the arts – so too are there differences between the contexts in which education work takes place – for example from music tuition in school or university, to music therapy in the health sector, to private

Table 2. Graduates' education occupations.

Occupation	% Creative graduates ($n = 151$)[a]
Music Teacher (Private Tuition)	19.21
University Lecturer	11.92
University Tutor	9.93
Dance Teacher (Private Tuition)	9.93
Secondary School Teacher	9.27
Teacher of English to Speakers of Other Languages	2.65
Primary School Teacher	1.99
Private Tutors and Teachers Not Otherwise Classified	1.99
Vocational Education Teacher (Aus)/Polytechnic Teacher (NZ)	1.32
Education Reviewer	0.66
Drama Teacher (Private Tuition)	0.66
'Teacher' – but did not specify level of detail required for further classification	30.46

[a]Eight people did not provide information beyond 'education', so have not been included in this table.

tuition, to community music practices. As the latter group of examples shows, there are also differences between 'arts education' (e.g. musical instrument tuition, or the teaching of painting) and 'arts in education' (e.g. the use of music to teach mathematics, or film to teach a foreign language). All of these examples highlight the complexity of creative work in education. In this article we argue that it is only possible to chart and quantify this complexity through the use of a range of data sources and approaches.

'Top-down' approaches and their limits

As part of long-term and ongoing research that seeks to better understand the creative workforce, the CCI developed the metaphor of the 'Creative Trident'. Drawing on data from the Australian census, the CCI developed an occupation/industry matrix of two rows and two columns (Figure 1).

The Trident defines creative employment as: those in creative occupations in the creative industries (who are termed 'core' or 'specialist' creative workers); those in creative occupations outside the creative industries ('embedded' creative workers); and those in non-creative roles within the creative industries ('support' workers). The fourth quadrant contains the balance of the workforce: all of those employed in non-creative occupations outside the creative industries. As one of the Trident's architects, Stuart Cunningham, observes, 'Simply put, the number of people employed in the "creative economy": is the total of creative industries employment plus embedded employment' (2013, 128).

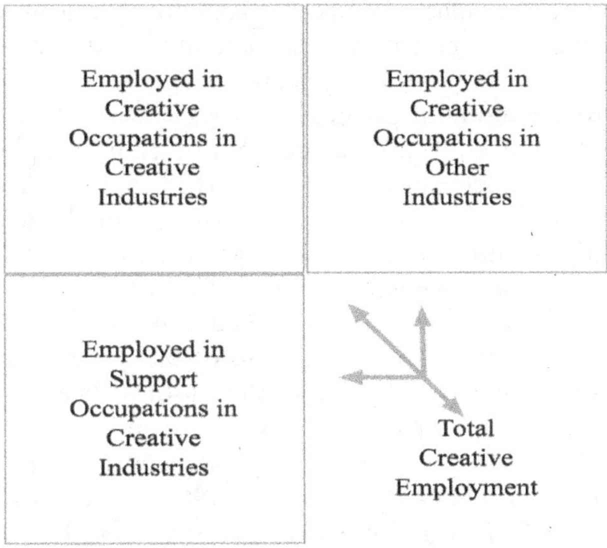

Figure 1. The Creative Trident model: mapping creative occupations and industries.

'Top-down' approaches which use census data to draw conclusions about the size of the creative workforce, such as the Trident, do not however reveal the whole picture of creative employment in education. Such approaches, we argue, need to be supplemented and extended by 'bottom-up' approaches, such as graduate tracking surveys, in order for the contribution made to the education sector by creative workers or workers with creative qualifications to be more accurately evaluated and assessed. The reasons for this are several. A national census provides a snapshot of employment on a particular day in a particular country. Respondents detail their occupation based on their main income at the time of the survey. This will affect the calculation of (embedded creative) employment in several ways. First, the increasing number of creative and other workers who work in several jobs simultaneously will only be represented in the census in one occupation and industry segment. An artist or musician who earns their main income from their creative work but who also has a part-time, casual or sessional teaching job, for example, will only appear in the census in their core creative occupation. Second, those creative workers who are employed as administrators, teachers, lecturers or researchers in formal primary, secondary or tertiary institutions, or in informal settings, must decide whether to represent themselves as teachers etc., or to list their occupation as their creative specialisation, within the education segment. In either case, the census data will not pick up all of those who are either embedded creative workers, or who have creative industries training or backgrounds and are earning their main income from a non-creative occupation. That is to say, the census data available to us is likely to significantly misrepresent embedded creative employment in education. It is still instructive to examine this data, but this caveat must be acknowledged.

We know from bottom-up graduate surveys such as *Creative Graduates Creative Futures* (Ball et al. 2010), the US Strategic National Arts Alumni Project (SNAAP) (Lindemann and Tepper 2012), and the Australian survey we discuss in more detail in the second part of this article, that many graduates with creative qualifications or backgrounds in the creative industries work as education professionals – administrators, teachers, lecturers or researchers – in non-creative areas. As noted above, census data alone will not necessarily accurately represent the size of this group. Neither will census data alone tell us whether these education professionals are or ever have been also employed in a creative occupation. A significant proportion of this group is likely to be primary school teachers, who are typically generalist teachers. Given that in many countries generalist teachers tend to teach arts at primary level (Alter, Hays, and O'Hara 2009; EACEA 2009), whereas specialist arts teachers are often employed to teach arts subjects at secondary level, those generalist primary teachers with qualifications or backgrounds in the creative industries are unlikely to be represented as embedded creatives in censuses, despite the fact that they undertake creative work as part of their normal employment. The extent to which these workers' qualifications or backgrounds inform or define their roles in education can only be discerned via targeted surveys, such as *Creative Graduates* – the large Australian study of graduate destinations which we discuss in the second part of this article.

A further difficulty in enumerating the embedded creative workforce in education relates to creative workers whose employment in education not only represents part of their career portfolio, but is also for a limited period of time. Partnerships between creative workers, arts and cultural organisations and educators in both formal and informal educational settings are numerous, and take many different forms around the world (IFACCA 2012). Artist-in-residence programmes facilitated by state arts agencies in partnership with education authorities, or by independent organisations, such as the Leverhulme Trust in the UK, may run for short periods and be based around a particular creative project. Other examples include the Arts Victoria Artists in Schools programme in which artists work in schools for up to 20 days at a time (Arts Victoria 2011).

Collaborations between artists and educators may take place over a more extended period of time, such as the Enquiry Schools and Change Schools programmes delivered under the UK Creative Partnerships scheme (2002–2011). Enquiry Schools was a one-year programme, and Change Schools was a three-year programme, although the actual time spent in schools by 'Creative Agents' was limited to six days in the former programme, and 20 days in the latter.

Exposure-to-arts programmes involving school excursions to galleries or arts centres, or incursions delivered by visiting arts organisations in schools, also involve creative workers in education activities (Arts Victoria 2011). In addition, creative workers may also be employed for short periods to provide professional development activities for teachers. This is considered to be particularly important at primary level (Bowell 2011), although once again data on the number of creative workers engaged in such work is limited and dispersed.

From 'top-down' to 'bottom-up' approaches to creative work in education

Despite these caveats, census data can provide some insights into the creative workforce in education. CCI analysis of Australian census data for 2006 and 2011 indicates that of those respondents self-identifying as working in creative occupations, a total of 10,924 creative workers were embedded in primary, secondary, tertiary and adult education in 2006, growing to 13,134 in 2011. This represents 7.39% of the total number of embedded creative workers in 2006, and 8.11% of the total in 2011. In both census periods considerably larger numbers of creative workers were recorded as embedded in tertiary education than in pre-school and school age education, or in adult education. As we will discuss further below, this finding was a little surprising given the volume of literature on arts education in schools, compared with the relatively small literature on tertiary arts education.

This finding also appears to contrast with that of the UK *Creative Graduates Creative Futures* survey (which is discussed in more detail below), in which fewer than 1% of respondents indicated that they were teaching at the tertiary level at the time of the survey (Ball et al. 2010, 114). This apparent anomaly may be explained by the fact that the majority of respondents who were teaching at the time of the UK survey 'recorded their job title as teacher and did not specify the level at which they were teaching' (Ball et al. 2010, 114). That is, it is conceivable that many of those creative graduates who recorded their occupation simply as 'teacher' were working in higher education.

In both the 2006 and 2011 Australian censuses, 'Librarian' was the occupation with the largest number of embedded workers in each of the three education segments. Librarians embedded in education represented 42% of the total number of embedded Librarians in 2006, and 44.97% in 2011. There were also substantial numbers of Public Relations Professionals, Marketing Specialists, Software Developer Programmers and Instrumental Musicians working in primary, secondary, tertiary or adult education. But while these occupations are classed as creative occupations in Australia, they are not all recognised as such in other countries. This highlights one of the difficulties in accurately comparing data from one country to another: occupational and industry codes and descriptors are rarely commensurable.

There is a wealth of the literature from many different countries on arts education, and the importance of the arts in education.[1] Much of this literature focuses on the processes, impacts or outcomes of teaching the arts or creativity, with some attention paid to the training and expertise of teachers. While often not their primary concern, some reports and studies do provide detailed statistics and insights into the educational backgrounds of teachers, and the professional development activities available to them. Although the data and discussions rarely directly address our focus here (enumerating and evaluating the embedded creative workforce in education), they do indirectly allow us to tease out some of the dynamics of embedded creative work in education in a variety of countries. In the United States, for example, the National Centre for Education Statistics (NCES) has conducted three surveys of arts education in public elementary and secondary schools (1994–1995, 1999–2000, 2009–2010). *Inter alia*, these surveys examine the types of arts instructors employed to provide arts education instruction, the provision of professional development for arts teachers and their participation in professional development activities, and the time spent on teaching, planning and preparation. In 2009–2010, among public elementary schools that offered instruction in various arts subjects, 91% employed music specialists, 84% employed visual arts specialists, 57% employed dance specialists, and 42% employed drama/theatre specialists (NCES 2012, 6). In elementary schools, most music specialists (88%) and most visual arts specialists (83%) taught the subjects full-time (NCES 2012, 8). In public secondary schools for the school year 2008–2009, 81% of the estimated 65,800 music instructors were full-time specialists, with a further 15% being part-time specialists. Of the estimated 49,700 visual arts instructors, 86% were full time specialists, and 8% part-time specialists. Of the estimated 5,600 dance instructors, 56% were full-time specialists and 13% part-time specialists. And for drama/theatre, full-time specialists made up 64% of the estimated 18,000 total, with 9% part-time specialists (NCES 2012, 11). The proportion of full-time specialist arts teachers in both public elementary and secondary schools increased in all of these arts forms from the 1999–2000 survey to the most recent, but since the total numbers cited here are estimates, we can at best only estimate the proportion of the total teaching cohort that these embedded creative workers represent. There are several further complications. The first relates to a calculation of the total number of secondary public school teachers. The US Bureau of Labour Statistics Occupational Employment Statistics only provides a combined total for public *and* private secondary school teachers (1,091,710 in 2009), while the NCES survey only covers public school teachers.[2] The second complication relates to the fact that substantial numbers of full-time arts teachers taught at more than one school (NCES 2012, 18, 24, 32, 37).

Despite these limitations, we can gain more detailed insights into the creative workforce in education from bottom-up studies such as those by the

NCES than from census data alone. In other US research, the 2010 SNAAP survey of 10,975 arts graduates found that 12% were employed at the time of the survey as Arts Educators in primary or secondary schools, with a further 2% listing their occupation as 'other Arts Educator'. In the CCI framework, these respondents would be classified as embedded creative workers. In addition to these embedded creatives, 6% of respondents to the SNAAP survey reported working in 'Education, Training, Library' occupations outside the arts. These workers would not be counted as creatives under the Creative Trident methodology because they are not directly working in a creative occupation.

Another recent graduate survey provides a range of data and information about the creative workforce in education in the UK. Fully one-third of the 3457 respondents to the *Creative Graduates Creative Futures* survey reported that they had taught in some capacity at primary, secondary or tertiary level since graduation (Ball et al. 2010, 113). At the time of the survey, 13.4% of those reporting current main work activity were teaching and research professionals, with 5.5% identifying as teachers of any arts/crafts/media/design/performing arts subject (Ball et al. 2010, Appendix 6, 123). Overall, 18% of those reporting 'any current activity' (including part-time or voluntary work in up to three activities) were in teaching occupations (Ball et al. 2010, Appendix 6, 126). Women and older graduates (over 40) were more likely to have worked as a teacher in a creative art and design subject (Ball et al. 2010, 113). In response to the question 'what kind of career did you aspire to [when you finished your undergraduate degree course]', only 7.4% nominated teaching, and only 4.2% nominated teaching in an arts/crafts/media/design/performing arts subject (Ball et al. 2010, Appendix 6, 183). One in ten graduates had studied for a teaching qualification since completing their undergraduate studies, although only 59% of these were currently working as a teacher at the time of the survey. Teaching or research was the fourth most popular career goal upon graduation, but the second largest occupation at the time of the survey (Ball et al. 2010, Appendix 6, 185). This finding underscores the importance of the education sector for creative graduates in the UK.

Creative graduates and employment in education in Australia

Current literature paints a dismal picture of the career outcomes of creative graduates in Australia, based largely on short-term and broad-brush measurements of the graduate outcomes of creative and performing arts courses. Annual Australian graduate destination research reports that 48.3% of tertiary creative/performing arts graduates are employed full-time, and 51.7% are seeking employment three to four months after course completion, whereas 71.3% of university graduates in general are employed full-time, and 29.4% are looking for work (Graduate Careers Australia 2013). The main reason for this pattern of early unemployment appears to be that demand for graduate level work in creative arts occupations exceeds supply (Menger 2006). The conventional narrative on careers in the arts suggests that only a very few of the most brilliant, determined and/or lucky graduates will succeed. The vast majority of graduate creative and performing artists are expected to experience an extended transition period from education to work characterised by unemployment and underemployment. Most are expected to end up employed in a wide variety of other arts-related and non-arts-related employment scenarios.

Existing empirical work in Australia investigating graduate outcomes tends however to suffer from significant conceptual and methodological problems. These problems mean that it has not thus far been possible to paint a sufficiently nuanced picture of creative arts career outcomes and trajectories. First, existing graduate tracking research aggregates the disciplines of design, media and the arts for reporting purposes to maximise simplicity, and sometimes also includes the humanities (Graduate Careers Australia 2013). Arguably, each of these disciplines has distinct career patterns and challenges. Second, like the national census, existing studies of graduate destinations focus on the graduate's 'main source of employment', and ignore portfolio career patterns, self-employment and multiple job-holding, all of which are common experiences for creative graduates. These studies tend to synonymise the seeking of *more* work (as is common in the portfolio career pattern and/or self-employment), with *being unemployed* and seeking *any* work. Third, existing research tends not to pursue the graduate career trajectory far enough. As demonstrated in Cunningham and Bridgstock's (2012) research into the career paths of media, communication and cultural studies graduates, and in McCowan and Wyganowska's (2008) telephone surveys with creative industries graduates at Queensland University of Technology, it can take two to three years for creative graduates to 'settle' into careers. Research which tracks graduate career outcomes over a shorter time period is then not likely to provide a realistic picture of creative graduates' career outcomes and trajectories. Fourth, there has been little systematic investigation into the individual contextual factors (e.g. graduate capability), or educational-developmental experiences associated with early career success or sectoral/occupational exits among creative graduates (c.f. Bridgstock 2011). Fifth, existing research does not explore the various kinds of creative value that creative graduates add through their work, whether or not they or their work are categorised as 'creative'.

The study discussed in the remainder of this article characterises the trajectories, experiences and destinations of Australian creative arts graduates to five years of post-course completion. It takes account of portfolio career configurations, and time needed to 'settle' into creative careers. It is limited; however, in that the sample corresponds with the 'cultural production' category of the CCI Trident Mark II model of creative workforce

(1) mean = 4.17 (SD = 1.11) and mean = 4.12 (SD = 1.19), respectively, and (2) mean = 2.90 (SD = 1.25) and 2.85 (SD = 1.32), respectively). Full-time and casually employed educators were somewhat less likely than part-time and self-employed educators to aspire to creative careers (χ^2 (4) = 10.40, $p = 0.034$). The majority of casually employed educators were university tutors engaging in concurrent further study. Music graduates were most likely to be self-employed as educators; performing arts graduates were mostly likely to be employed full-time as educators (χ^2 (20) = 51.08, $p = 0.0001$).

These findings indicate that creative graduates who teach do so for different reasons. For a proportion of (typically) self-employed or part-time teachers, most commonly with backgrounds in music, education appears to be a 'day job', with graduates maintaining concurrent creative career aspirations. On the other hand, there are a group of (typically) full-time or casually employed teachers, most commonly with backgrounds in performing arts/dance, where creative career aspirations are less likely to be maintained.

Adding creative value and career satisfaction/success

All survey participants who were engaged in non-creative work were asked to indicate, on a 1–5 scale, to what extent they felt that they added creative value in their non-creative work. Overall, the mean rating given was 4.01 (SD = 1.28). Compared with other non-creative work, graduates employed as educators indicated much higher ratings with respect to adding creative value, at mean = 4.50 (SD = 1.17) vs. mean = 3.89 (SD = 1.29), $U = -3.97$, $p = 0.0001$. The most common types of creative value that graduates employed as educators felt that they added included as follows: imagination/creative viewpoint/creative ideas (40.88%); critical thinking (37.12%); public speaking/presentation/performance (32.70%); and writing/editing (27.67%).

In general graduates who only did creative work felt that they were more successful than those who did non-creative work ($U = 4.57$, $p = 0.0001$, 1–5 mean = 3.66 SD = 1.07 vs. mean = 3.23 SD = 1.20). However, graduates who engaged in education work rated themselves as more successful, on average, than those who only worked in creative jobs ($U = -2.22$, $p = 0.028$, 1–5 mean = 3.78 SD = 0.95 vs. mean = 3.61 SD = 0.90). This finding may be partly explained by the reasonably strong positive correlation of 0.402 ($p = 0.01$) between the extent to which graduates in education believed that they added creative value through their non-creative work, and their self-rated career success.

Conclusion

The Australian graduate tracking survey has provided a wealth of findings that expand previous census-based analysis of creative employment in

Australia, and in particular creative employment in the education sector. First, the survey findings confirm that education qualifications and education work are both very common indeed among cultural production graduates – in fact, nearly one quarter of the creative graduates surveyed were engaged in education work to some extent at the time of surveying. Education work seems to be a good option for creative graduates, in that those who undertake education work are satisfied with their careers – more so than graduates who undertake other types of 'non-creative' work, and interestingly, also more than those who only undertake creative work. This may be related to the fact that the educators in the sample feel that they add creative value through their education work.

However, creative graduates who pursue creative work are not a homogeneous group. It is clear from the findings of the study that creative graduates pursue education work for different reasons. For some (music graduates in particular), education work seems to be a 'day job' phenomenon, undertaken on a self-employment basis at the same time as creative work and creative career building. For others (particularly performing arts graduates), education work seems to be more than a 'day job'. For these graduates, education work is undertaken as a career.

Some findings from the survey analyses are not consistent with the census analysis results, and further investigation is required. For instance, a considerably larger proportion of respondents to the graduate survey who were working in creative jobs (specialist, embedded, support) were working in specialist creative occupations (64.32%) than census findings would suggest. In the 2011 census, only 28.06% of creative jobs were in specialist creative occupations. And, relatedly, a considerably smaller proportion of graduates working in creative occupations were working in embedded creative occupations (20.70%) than might have been expected, going on analysis of census data. In the 2011 census, 30.34% of creative jobs were embedded in industries outside the creative industries.

There may be several explanations for these differences. First, the Trident statistics include creative services occupations (e.g. design, advertising and marketing), and it may be these creatives who are overwhelmingly embedded in education industries, rather than cultural production creatives. Another explanation may be that the incidence of embedded cultural production work in education may be much higher among established creative workers (e.g. via 'artists in schools initiatives') rather than graduates zero to seven years after course completion. Third, the Australian census only collects data with respect to the respondent's 'main job', whereas the data reported here pertains to all jobs that the participants held. Embedded work may be relatively more likely to be reported as a 'main job' in the census than specialist work, as embedded workers are employees and are more likely to be full-time than specialist creative workers (who have a tendency to be self-employed).

The graduate survey also provides some insights in to the contributions that creative graduates make to the education sector, which census data cannot speak to directly. As previously mentioned, education occupations represented the highest concentration of non-creative jobs held by the graduates, with the majority working as 'Education Professionals'. Despite the fact that most of this group were working in 'Arts Education' (35.76% of education professionals, 7.93% of all employed) – principally as private music, dance or drama teachers – they are not counted as embedded creative workers (or indeed as creative workers at all) under the census/Trident methodology. Rather, they are regarded as 'non-creative workers working in non-creative industries'. The survey approach is able to investigate in a more fine grained way than the census analysis the contributions of occupations throughout the creative value chain, including those for whom the key output may be thought of as 'creative workers' rather than 'creative work'. This points to a potential shortcoming of the Creative Trident methodology: by specifying creative economy employment as only including specialist, embedded and support work, other workers who are necessary to the operation and growth of the creative economy – such as those who educate and train creative workers – are missed.

The second insight that the graduate survey provides beyond the census analysis, is the extent to which those working in non-creative jobs added creative value. Graduates employed as educators in particular indicated very high ratings, with the most common types of creative value added including imagination/creative viewpoint/creative ideas; critical thinking; public speaking/presentation/performance; and writing/editing. These findings indicate that workers with creative training or backgrounds do perceive themselves to be making substantial creative contributions in jobs classified as 'non-creative'. These contributions cannot currently be revealed in top-down approaches, such as analysis of census data, but rather can only be recognised in bottom-up approaches such as graduate surveys. In combination, top-down and bottom-up approaches can provide a range of insights not only into the phenomenon of embedded creative work in the education sector, but in to the variety of contributions that creative workers, or those with creative training, can make to education.

Notes

1. See, for example, UNESCO (2013).
2. Bureau of Labour Statistics (2009).
3. Using the Creative Trident 2011 classification of creative vs. non-creative jobs.

References

Alter, F., T. Hays, and R. O'Hara. 2009. "Creative Arts Teaching and Practice: Critical Reflections of Primary School Teachers in Australia." *International Journal of Education and the Arts* 10 (9): 1–21.

Arts Victoria. 2011. *Partnerships between Schools and the Professional Arts Sector: Evaluation of Impact on Student Outcomes*. Melbourne: Arts Victoria.

Australian Bureau of Statistics. 2014. "1292.0 – Australian and New Zealand Standard Industrial Classification (ANZSIC), 2006 (Revision 1.0)." Accessed August 3, 2014. http://www.abs.gov.au/AUSSTATS/abs@.nsf/Previousproducts/3A98B8464571A054CA25711F001470B8?opendocument

Ball, L., E. Pollard, and N. Stanley. 2010. *Creative Graduates, Creative Futures*. Brighton: Creative Graduates, Creative Futures, Higher Education Partnership and the Institute for Employment Studies.

Bowell, I. 2011. "Supporting Visual Art Teaching in Primary Schools." *Australian Art Education* 34 (2): 98–118.

Bridgstock, R. 2011. "Skills for Creative Industries Graduate Success." *Education & Training* 53 (1): 9–26.

Bureau of Labor Statistics. 2009. Secondary School Teachers, Except Special and Vocational Education. *Occupational Employment and Wages* May: 25–2031. Accessed December 6, 2013. http://www.bls.gov/oes/2009/may/oes252031.htm

Cunningham, S. 2013. *Hidden Innovation: Policy, Industry and the Creative Sector*. St Lucia: University of Queensland Press.

Cunningham, S., and R. Bridgstock. 2012. "Say Goodbye to the Fries: Graduate Careers in Media, Cultural and Communication Studies." *Media International Australia: Incorporating Culture and Policy* 145: 145–160.

EACEA. 2009. *Arts and Cultural Education at School in Europe*. Brussels: EACEA.

Graduate Careers Australia. 2013. *GradStats: Employment and Salary Outcomes of Recent Higher Graduates 2013*. Parkville: Graduate Careers Australia.

IFACCA. 2012. *Creative Intersections: Partnerships between the Arts*. Sydney: Culture and Other Sectors.

Lindemann, D. J., and S. J. Tepper. 2012. *Painting with Broader Strokes: Reassessing the Value of an Arts Degree Based on the Results of the 2010 Strategic*

National Arts Alumni Project. Bloomington: Indiana University and Vanderbilt University, Strategic National Arts Alumni Project.

Mallon, M. 1999. "Going 'Portfolio': Making Sense of Changing Careers." *Career Development International* 4 (7): 358–370.

McCowan, C., and J. Wyganowska. 2008. "Gathering the Real Data from Creative Industries Graduates One Year Out." *Australian Journal of Career Development* 17 (1): 29–40.

Menger, P. M. 2006. Artistic Labor Markets: Contingent Work, Excess Supply and Occupational Risk Management. In *Handbook on the Economics of Art and Culture* 1, edited by V. A. Ginsburg and D. Throsby, 765–811. Oxford: Elsevier.

NCES (National Centre for Education Statistics). 2012. *Arts Education in Public Elementary and Secondary Schools 1999–2000 and 2009–10*. Washington, DC: NCES.

Throsby, C. D., and V. Hollister. 2003. *Don't Give Up Your Day Job: An Economic Study of Professional Artists in Australia*. Sydney: Australia Council for the Arts.

UNESCO. 2013. *Arts Education*. Accessed December 6, 2013. http://www.unesco.org/new/en/culture/themes/creativity/arts-education/

Creative work careers: pathways and portfolios for the creative economy

Daniel Ashton

Department of Film, Media and Creative Computing, School of Humanities and Cultural Industries, Bath Spa University, Bath, UK

This article examines the career opportunities, challenges and trajectories of creative work. As part of the Creative Trident approach to creative workforce measurements, the embedded mode draws attention to creative work as it is undertaken outside of the creative industries. This article further considers and conceptualises the complex careers pathways of creative workers. Firstly, creative workers in non-creative occupations in other industries are discussed to highlight the challenges and barriers to securing creative employment and the balance creative workers establish with other forms of employment. Secondly, students from creative courses going into non-creative occupations in other industries are discussed to highlight challenges students face in making the transition from higher education to creative employment in terms of workforce expectations and the competition amongst graduates. This article critically evaluates assumptions about transitions from education into creative work employment and associated career trajectories.

Introduction

In December 2010, Universities UK published *Creating Prosperity: The Role of Higher Education in Driving the UK's Creative Economy*, a report that emphasised higher education as the 'primary producer of the talent and skills that feed the creative industries' (iii). The report goes on to outline that:

> [...] the primary purpose of higher education is not to develop narrow skill sets [...] Higher education nurtures and develops creative talent, and produces graduates with deep specialism and, increasingly, the ability to work in multi-disciplinary teams. It is this talent that will innovate new products, processes

> and business models to drive the creative economy of the future. (Universities UK 2010a, v)

This talent-based approach is well established within a UK policy context and clear connections can be made to the earlier creative economy report *Creative Britain* (Department of Culture, Media and Sport [DCMS] 2008), in which a talent pathway is established through several stages of education. These reports sit within a wider policy context entwining higher education and the creative economy (see Banks and Hesmondhalgh 2009; Ashton and Noonan 2013). Central to these creative industries policy interventions is the question of how creativity and creative talent can, through higher education, be positioned as contributing to the UK economy. For Oakley, the global growth of the cultural and creative industries has seen this relationship become 'more formal, more directed and more calculating' (2013, 26).

Examining the distinctive features of creative work, Flew connects together individual understandings of creativity with workforce opportunities:

> The capacity to be creative is something that is highly regarded. It is seen as being part of what makes us human, and a creative society is seen as something worth aspiring to. From such an angle, it would appear that creativity, like culture, is something that you cannot have too much of. There is also ample evidence that the ability to pursue creative work is highly sought after (2012, 100)

These comments provide a helpful starting point in highlighting the different investments in creative production that extend from the capacity to be creative and involved in creative content production to making a living from, and contributing to, the economy as a creative worker. Reports, such as *Creative Britain* (DCMS 2008) and *Creating Prosperity* (Universities UK 2010a), and higher education practice underpinned by an 'industry-ready' employability agenda (see Ashton and Noonan 2013) address this later stage of enabling students to develop their interest in creative production and pursue careers as creative workers. However, as this article argues, there are potential obstacles for individuals moving positions on the talent pathway and in following a creative career trajectory.

Creative work is characterised by portfolio working, in which individuals are involved in 'multiple work and/or development activities simultaneously' (Pollard 2013, 54) and, as such, there exists a multiplicity of career pathways and trajectories. Conditions of portfolio working and 'multiple job-holding' (Throsby and Zednik 2011) are increasingly the norm within creative career and labour markets, and present a challenge for those hoping to secure creative occupations as a first choice and identify and follow defined career pathways and progression (see also, Stoyanova and Grugulis 2012 on career progression paradoxes). Building on a previous examination of the talent pathway approach of individuals realising and contributing their creativity to the economy (Ashton 2011a), this article draws on the concept of the 'embedded creative' to further examine the contingencies and challenges of a higher education for the creative industries.

Part one: defining (creative) industries and occupations

The concept of creativity is the focus of continued academic, industry and policy debate, and it has been constructed and identified in relation to specific industries (DCMS 2001) and as processes that can be seen across the economy (Potts and Cunningham 2008; Bakhshi, Freeman, and Higgs 2012). At stake within these debates are questions around what counts as creative work and who creative workers are. The Creative Trident approach – developed by the Australian Research Council Centre of Excellence for the Creative Industries and Innovation (CCI) (Higgs, Cunningham, and Bakhshi 2008; Cunningham 2011; Flew 2012) – is a conceptual and empirical resource for examining creative work. In introducing the Creative Trident approach, Flew (2012) surveys different workforce definitions and notes that due to a lack of agreed methodology, there has been a tendency to underestimate the number of people working in the creative industries. The Creative Trident approach emerged specifically in response to the Creative Industries National Mapping Project with the objective of 'provid[ing] "defensible"; evidence of the extent and contribution of creative workforce to the economy' (Higgs and Cunningham 2008, 3). As Higgs, Cunningham and Bakhshi outline, the Trident focuses on three types of employment, which collectively form the creative workforce:

> Specialist – artists, professionals or creative individuals working in the creative industries.
>
> Embedded – artists, professionals or creative individuals in creative roles 'embedded' in industries not defined as creative.
>
> Support – staff in the creative industries providing management, secretarial, administrative and accountancy back-up. (2008, 20)

The methodology for defining these categories is based around statistical classification analysis, but recognises that industry activity codes alone are insufficient (Cunningham 2013). As Cunningham (2013) outlines, the Trident disaggregates creative employment and allows for analysis of different types of employment (specialist, embedded and creative) and creative activity within different labour markets (notably between cultural production for final consumption and creative services as business-to-business activities). The Creative Trident approach considers occupational and industrial classifications highlighting that creative work is not always located within the creative industries. More specifically, the concept of 'embedded creative work' signals the diverse activities and locations associated with creative work and, for this discussion, raises some of the complexities of creative career trajectories from higher education into 'creative work in the creative industries'– specialist creative work.

Part two: the creative trident and diverse sites of cultural production

A portfolio career can involve a wide variety of 'creative' and 'non-creative' roles and contexts, and this article stresses the exploration of how 'creative workers' (see Hesmondhalgh and Baker 2011) and 'creative graduates' (see Ball, Pollard, and Stanley 2010) can find themselves in a variety of 'non-creative' roles and contexts.

Based on analysis of the wider inputs of creative work to the economy, Cunningham encourages a more nuanced account of where creative work takes place and argues that 'creatively trained people are more likely to be working outside the specialist creative industry sectors than inside them, and this is the case in most countries, and has been the case for a long time' (2011, 37). Whilst the embedded creative work approach importantly foregrounds other employment possibilities and highlights the creative worker undertaking *creative work* outside the creative industries, there is room to further examine the creative worker undertaking *non-creative* work and the associated career pathways and forms of portfolio working.

The Creative Trident approach emphasises the diversity of how and where creative work takes place. A number of commentators have taken the position that creative economy is suffused through all industries and that creative workers are embedded in all sectors to varying proportions (see Bakhshi, Freeman, and Higgs 2012 on the concept of 'creative intensities'; Hearn and Bridgstock 2014 for a wider outline). A revealing comparison may be drawn here with Negus' (2006) proposals on studying the creative/cultural industries like any other industries. On the one hand, Negus' perspective connects with the embedded creative work approach in looking outside of the creative industries to identify creative work. Indeed, Negus' takes issue with the idea that 'a cultural industry provides the main context within which cultural production takes place' (2006, 207). A reading of these comments in relation to the concept of embedded creative work might see this as a call to look beyond creative industries to other industries where creative work takes place. On the other hand, Negus questions the assumption of the inherent creativity of people and industries. For Negus, these industries should not be 'bracketed from the rest due to the particular type of artistic value or creativity that is *assumed* to reside there' (2006, 202; emphasis added). For example, the creative career portfolio of the creative worker undertaking administrative work with a creative industries company may be defined as much by the nature of the day-to-day income generating work, rather than their experiences as cultural producers or their wider creative contexts.

Noting the conditions and challenges of cultural labour markets, a pathway to non-creative work may be increasingly common for creative students graduating from higher education. As Oakley highlights, there is

> a growing body of evidence, about the nature of work in the creative industries and who gets it, the geographic distribution of such jobs [and] the deflation of the bubble of expectations about the growth in the creative industries themselves. (2013, 26)

For example, whilst creative graduates undertaking administrative work at a creative industries company would be included within a Creative Trident count of the creative workforce population, in terms of creative economy talent pathways and the kinds of *graduate* destinations that higher education institutions may be monitored on (see Higher Education Funding Council for England n.d.), the fit is less clear and not as might be expected. Returning to the *Creating Prosperity* report (Universities UK 2010a), this could see higher education creative graduates drawing on both specific occupational skills and wider generic skills to undertake ostensibly non-creative work in non-creative industries.

This article proposes addressing not just embedded creative work and creative workers in other contexts, but also creative workers in non-creative occupations in non-creative industries. This could be an understated aspect of the Creative Trident approach and include those who *could* contribute as creative workers, but do not count in either the specialist, embedded or support mode. Whilst there might be case for identifying such individuals as specialist workers who are concurrently undertaking work elsewhere as part of a portfolio career, a question mark emerges here around how meaningful (self)-definition can be given the frequency, duration and substance of creative work. Pursuing the theme of creative workers/students undertaking non-creative work presents a further dimension to the Creative Trident approach and indicates challenges facing those on the creative economy pathway. In putting forward the case for this extended analysis, part three focuses on creative workers in non-creative occupations in other industries and considers some of the challenges they face in securing and maintaining a creative work career. Part four then follows by considering students undertaking creative courses, who go on to work in non-creative occupations in other industries.

Part three: creative workers in non-creative occupations in other industries

In their discussion of creative cultural occupations outside the creative industries, Hearn and Bridgstock (2014, 44) comment on the relevance of self-definition to processes of classifying and measuring creative work:

> embedded creatives would not be categorized as such if they were not doing essentially the same work as those in creative firms. For example, a journalist outside the publishing industry must have described their work in such a way to be categorised as a journalist per se.

The following section addresses self-definition and those who could be regarded as creative workers, but whose career pathways and portfolio working practices mean that the status of creative work as a primary activity becomes uncertain. Exploration of these uncertain and tenuous positions can include the challenges and barriers to securing creative work (notably in the creative industries), and the push factors that see creative workers move career direction. These entry and exit strategies can be developed by also looking at the portfolio character of work and the extent to which descriptions of being a creative worker remain obvious and relevant when 'other' work is the main source of income and expenditure of time.

Challenges and barriers to creative occupations in the creative industries

In defining the creative industries, Hartley et al. refer to 'dynamic and volatile markets and industries' (2013, 65) and this section focuses on some of the labour market issues, challenges and barriers for finding 'creative work employment' and, especially for higher education students, of demonstrating 'employability for creative work'.

Challenges and barriers can be examined at a macro level, in which a complex range of factors interconnect to shape and constrain the possibilities for gaining creative work employment. Flew's (2012) engagement with established theories of unemployment is a useful reminder of the wider conceptual resources that may be drawn on in the analysis of creative work. Specifically, Flew (2012) outlines how theories of unemployment distinguish between frictional, structural and cyclical unemployment and that whilst analysis might focus on the challenges of creative labour workforce markets, these issues and processes can be identified across the economy more widely. With this in mind, the following turns to a number of commentators who have made significant contributions to analysing distinctive creative labour workforce conditions.

Reflecting on creative workforce issues in the UK, Haukka identifies:

> [...] an over-supply of new entrants, an agile freelance pool who must ensure their skill currency, a mismatch of applicants' skills to the needs of the job, new entrants finding it difficult to secure their first job, employers preferring to recruit experienced employees and freelancers from home and abroad, and new entrants lacking skills and knowledge in multi-platform content, intellectual property legislation, management and leadership, commercial acumen. (2010, 42)

This summary by Haukka captures many of the challenges and barriers to finding creative work employment and, within the scope of this article, why it is that creative workers may be faced with few alternatives but to seek employment in other industries, where the opportunities to undertake their core creative activities are not present.

Creative labour market conditions may also be addressed through questions of identity and those who are able to regularly secure employment. For example, issues of ethnic, gender and social underrepresentation have specifically been identified in relation to the creative industries (Creative and Cultural Skills 2008; see also: Allen et al. 2012; Lee 2013; Saha 2013). Issues of underrepresentation can also be considered as a question of 'fitting in' and, for Tomlinson (2007), the subjective dimensions of employability are continually overlooked within employability discourse. Tomlinson's analysis helps to reveal that barriers to creative employment can be explored in terms of attitudes, dispositions and identities. For example, part of the challenges in gaining access to creative employment may be networking norms, and Allen et al. examine how networking can act as 'a mechanism of social closure to the creative sector, favouring those with high levels of social and cultural capital' (2012, 10).

Further to networking practices that may be exclusionary in terms of social capital (Lee 2011) and the ability to manage competing personal and career commitments (Blair 2002), the ability to embody and perform recognisable creative worker identities is notable. Based on research into art colleges, Taylor and Littleton suggest in their discussion of creative identities that, 'it will be easier to be become accepted as an artist if you can look like one, that is, if you already are the same kind of person as other artists' (2012, 26). Likewise, Nixon and Crewe (2004) take up the issue of creative worker dispositions in their examination of advertising and magazine publishing. They note how certain aspects of 'cool' creative workplaces (see also McGuigan 2009; McRobbie 2002) can have a 'strongly gendered character' (2004, 134) and that 'the flourishing of robustly masculine cultures within agency offices and publishing companies formed a considerable block to women's capacity to succeed in these occupations' (2004, 146). They illustrate this culture through the examples of football in the corridor, condoms on the Christmas tree and Barbie dolls in bondage gear. In their closing remarks, Nixon and Crewe argue that 'the subjectivities of creative workers and the occupational cultures they inhabit mediate the practices of cultural production in which they are engaged' (2004, 146).

From Nixon and Crewe's analysis, at least two issues of relevance for this discussion can be drawn. Firstly, dominant forms of subjectivity and occupational cultures may provide barriers to working in the creative industries for those who identify themselves as creative workers but are unable to 'fit in'. Secondly, and with reference to creative workers embedded in other industries, creative worker attitudes and dispositions may differ within different occupational cultures. With both these points, it is clear that the possibilities for undertaking creative work cannot be separated from creative worker identities, workplace cultures and industry contexts. As the following section turns to, individuals may go to significant lengths to maintain these identities even when the opportunities to engage with creative workplaces and connect with established forms of creative worker identities and cultures are hard to come by.

Primary occupations

Examining the careers of artists in Australia, Bridgstock notes changes in traditional employment relations, and that, 'increasingly work can be characterised as a series of periods within and outside paid employment, linked by experiences of learning and retraining. In addition these periods of paid employment may include casual work, short-term contracts and job sharing' (2005, 41). The norm of temporary and freelance working practices in the creative industries is well established (Oakley 2008). Indeed, part of the distinctiveness of working in the embedded creative mode are the possibilities for greater security of tenure and more stable working conditions. Writing in relation to the Australian context also, Bennett addresses concurrent working and multiple job-holding and outlines how:

> artists meet their needs through acting in multiple concurrent roles and often combine high- and low-skilled positions as required [...] it is common to find artists working concurrently as a performer, director, manager, teacher, and in low-skilled administrative and technical roles. (2009, 312)

The list of occupations provided here resonates with what Throsby and Zednik (2011) would describe as arts-related work. The inclusion of low-skilled administrative work would though more readily connect with the non-arts labour categorisation of the type that Throsby and Zednik (2011) elaborate on through the adage of actors working as waiters and taxi drivers. In considering different motivations and preferences, they go on to suggest that arts-related work, 'might be deliberately chosen by artists as providing a new and stimulating way in which their creativity can be expressed, or as a more attractive source of additional income than driving a taxi' (Throsby and Zednik 2011, 19). The practices of multiple job-holding and the diversity of what can be involved in creative work portfolio careers indicate, for this discussion, the complexities of creative career pathways.

In investigating the notion of primary occupations, McRobbie's (2011) comments on the status of the second job are revealing. In reflecting on the career choices of a past student, McRobbie notes the irony and tension that creative workers, 'rely on a second job which is in effect a real job, even though it may be on a project or on a casual contract', and that 'many of the creatives find themselves earning the bulk of their income from the second job' (2011, 32). McRobbie goes on to suggest that her, 'research shows that such a strata of young people would be better off opting for the profession of the second job, and retraining to gain entitlements and status and promotion' (2011, 32). Along the same lines, Throsby and Zednik focus on non-arts labour markets and note that 'non-art work tends to be significantly more lucrative than an artist's creative work when judged per unit of time' (2011, 11), and that 'the factors preventing artists from reducing their non-arts commitment and devoting more time to creative work are overwhelmingly related to the economic circumstances in which artistic occupations are pursued' (2011, 13). Whilst both McRobbie (2011) and Throsby and Zednik (2011) consider the centrality of the second job, it is McRobbie (2011), who takes a step further in considering how non-creative occupations in other industries might be more than a stopgap or a means to piece together an income. That said, McRobbie (2011) goes on to argue that the myth of personal creativity is so dominant that many creative workers who rely on a second job for their income would forgo establishing careers, entitlement, status and promotion within this job. These observations have strong parallels with Marsden's (2007) analysis of 'entry tournaments' and the conditions in which aspirants for particular occupations continue to compete for opportunities that are closing down and thereby have to make do with precarious employment conditions.

These comments on the balance of occupational opportunities and directions add a further dimension to Throsby and Zednik's analysis of non-arts work, in which they consider the desirability and creative challenge of working in a creative role in non-creative industries:

> Given the evidence that a majority of artists prefer to work in their core-creative practice or in arts-related work, and only resort to non-arts work out of financial necessity, it is tempting to assume that looking for work outside the arts is always a second-best option. (2011, 19)

Whilst Throsby and Zednik are referring to undertaking arts-related creative activities (writing, visual art, craft, acting, dancing, music, composing, community cultural development), even if outside the arts, they raise interesting possibilities around what level of engagement and practice is significant for meaningful (self-)identifications of being a creative worker. The portfolio careers of creative workers are complex and assumptions that creative work always remains the core activity may be questioned – especially when it may be the case that 'other' work exists as the primary occupation and has a much stronger bearing on career identities.

Part of the rationale individuals might hold for investing in creative identities can include the status of these 'cool jobs' in 'hot industries' (Neff,

Wissinger, and Zukin 2005). For Taylor and Littleton, 'some creative workers may be engaged in a project of avoidance and turning away from workplaces and careers which are interpreted in terms of a caricature modernist industry and the lives associated with it' (2012, 141). They go on to highlight:

> [...] an important direction for future research will be to ask more questions about alternative occupations which are being avoided, and about the sources of common understandings or perceptions of *other* work, and contemporary life more generally, as inevitably unsatisfying, over-systematized and uncreative. (Taylor and Littleton 2012, 141)

The approach taken in this article has strong connections with Taylor and Littleton's proposed research direction, with the difference here being that creative workers might explicitly take the step away from not only the creative industries, as with embedded creative workers, but also from creative work. Continuing this discussion, the next section explores the transitions that students can make from higher education into creative work.

Part four: students from creative courses in non-creative occupations in other industries

This section considers students on creative courses that go on to work in non-creative occupations in other industries, and examines the links between creative degree courses (see Ball, Pollard, and Stanley 2010) and creative occupations. The relationship between creative work and higher education can most readily be identified with the talent pathway approach of *Creative Bath* introduced at the outset (DCMS 2008; see also Ashton 2011a) and the industry-focused, employability agenda of higher education delivering creative industries-related degree courses (see Ashton and Noonan 2013). A major contention of this article has been the complexities of such pathways – a perspective that builds on Haukka's (2010) discussion of how creative industries' education-to-work transitions are not institutionally or occupationally determined compared to pathways into other industries. In illustrating this, Haukka (2010) points to extended transition periods, multiple entry attempts and employment within and outside the creative industries (see also Bridgstock 2005). Developing Cunningham's (2011) earlier comments on creatively trained people as more likely to be working outside specialist creative industry sectors, this formulation draws attention to creatively trained people, who neither work in the creative industries or in embedded creative employment. Rather, this analysis specifically highlights the tensions and complexities of the higher education to creative economy talent pathway.

In their discussion of the steps that a music student makes in becoming 'professional', Creech et al. (2008) describe transition as a process, rather than an event. They go on to consider how the process of transition, 'opens up a space in the imagination where the individual has the capacity to anticipate future possibilities in relation to present action and to begin to develop effective coping strategies for dealing with real or imagined challenges lying ahead' (Creech et al. 2008, 316). In relation to higher education students, 'present action' may be understood as their degree programme and their university experience, and future possibilities as the career pathways they may pursue. Creech et al. (2008) conclude their study by noting the challenges higher education institutions face in supporting students seeking both performance and alternative careers. This recognition of different career possibilities is central to expressing how expected trajectories and pathways are contingent and continually negotiated.

The changing workforce profile of the creative industries is particularly important for considering how higher education connects with working in the creative industries. Data compiled by Creative Skillset (2009) show that graduates now make up 73% of the workforce, compared to 66% in 2003. This changing workforce profile can be linked to 'an increase of 150% between 1999/2000 and 2008/2009' in students enrolling on media studies degrees, with creative arts and design degrees also showing a significant increase (64% overall) (Universities UK 2010b, 27). Within this context, there are initiatives that seek to develop understanding of recruitment and training needs for the creative industries (for example, in the UK, see Creative Skillset n.d. and in Australia, see CCI n.d.). Within the UK, Creative Skillset (n.d.) positions its research and evaluation strategy in relation to the demand-led system set out in the Leitch Review, in which employer voice is paramount. This approach is not without criticism, with Brown, Hesketh, and Williams suggesting that a major weakness of this 'consensus position' of government and employers is that it 'presents employability as a technical problem of ensuring that labour market entrants have the skill sets that match the requirements of employers' (2003, 116). Gaining a handle on the requirements of employers and industry more widely, especially given the strong prevalence of freelance working patterns, can be a significant challenge.

Workforce expectations

The links between higher education and the creative industries are complex and varied. For example, Creative and Cultural Skills (2007, 60 cited in Haukka 2010, 59–60) refer to, 'an extraordinarily complex array of qualifications purporting to service the creative and cultural sector [...] driven by the appeal of the sector to young people and the interest in learning creative subjects within schools, Further and Higher Education'. This array of qualifications can be linked to uncertainty around their specific connections with creative careers pathways. On this, Haukka (2010) and Guile (2010) consider the growth in higher education courses and associated industry expectations. Haukka (2010) notes that qualifications do not provide a guarantee of workforce entry and for Guile, despite the close links between universities and industries, studying for a degree related to the creative industries 'rarely provides an expectation or understanding of what is required in vocational contexts' (2010, 470). Similarly, for Bennett (2009), qualifications are not seen as requirements for the performing arts, where practical experience is highly valued. These perspectives reveal the complexities of the education-to-industry transitions within the creative industries, and that, for those at the boundaries and intersections of higher education and the creative industries, there may be prolonged periods of uncertainty and negotiation.

Part of the challenge of connecting education with creative work remains the gap between employer and industry norms, and the expectations and the understandings of such creative employment that students are able to gain through their degree. Haukka (2010) documents a three-year study investigating the education, training and work experiences based around a survey of aspiring creative workers and employers. From this survey, Haukka noted that, 'many respondents to the aspiring creatives survey perceived themselves as having very good employability skills and job-specific skills contrary to the reported views of employers that graduates are not industry ready' (2010, 46). Under the subheading, 'meeting skills needs of employers', Haukka summarises from the employer survey that 'employers indicated the capabilities of aspiring creatives for all 15 skills and attributes included in the employer survey were below their expectations when compared to the level of importance they placed on these skills and attributes to their workplace' (2010, 49). The existence of such gaps, to whatever extent they are perceived and constructed by different parties, can be further understood and anticipated, thanks to research on the embedded creative work mode. In indicating a breadth of potential sites for creative employment, the Creative Trident research also indicates an even greater breadth of recruitment norms and expectations both within and beyond the creative industries. The challenge of this can be connected with the above discussion in which employability for creative work was raised. Bennett's research on arts graduates also raises this point around how students would be able to engage with and then go on to demonstrate creative work identities:

> For performing arts graduates the need for a positive and broadly based professional identity is clear. Unfortunately, role models are most often successful performance artists, and there is a very real risk that students' performance identities preclude them from planning a positive engagement with non-performance activities. (2009, 313)

The importance of identity to the transitions that students may make from education into creative employment is instructively captured here and, in relation to the embedded creative work mode, there is a need to consider the different kinds of occupational cultures and identities that students are able to encounter and then go on to embody and/or perform.

This question of industry requirements and expectations are compounded for students by the labour market challenges they face. For those who continue to aspire to secure creative employment but are unable to, either within specialist or embedded modes of creative work, an uncertain process of navigating unexpected pathways can ensue. This differs to the circumstances that Cunningham is able to outline whereby the challenges of working in the creative industries may be obviated through working as an embedded creative (2011). Cunningham suggests that working within the embedded creative work mode and outside of the creative industries could be seen as a career preference and strategy to avoid precarity. For those unable to secure creative employment in either specialist or embedded modes, a profile of multiple job-holding and crossing occupational boundaries is common. This could be extended 'entry tournaments' (Stoyanova and Grugulis 2012), prolonged work as an intern (Carrot Workers Collective 2011) and/or engaging in forms of peripheral participation in trying to develop a reputation and secure positions of greater responsibility (Grugulis and Stoyanova 2011), whilst securing a main income elsewhere – for example, in 'other' occupations as highlighted by Throsby and Zednik (2011). These scenarios of internship and peripheral participation are more specific to students, graduates and earlier career entrants and emphasise the need to include the potential in-between and overlap activities in any account of workforce mapping and career transitions.

Pedagogical research initiatives have examined the intersections of industry and education and the place of work-related simulated learning environments (see Ashton 2013b), work placements (Berger, Wardle, and Zezulkova 2013) and career development strategies (Bridgstock 2011). A concern for how students are able to gain relevant insights has been documented as something that students also raise. For example, in Bennett's survey of performing arts, the most common response provided by student on the changes that they would make to their education and training included, 'open discussion about the realities of working life and the limited performance opportunities' (2009, 320). The realities of working life as posed here connect with the reference to 'real and imagined challenges' by Creech et al. (2008) and the coping strategies noted by Ball, Pollard, and Stanley (2010). Engaging students with issues of unstable employment conditions is not a case of 'smashing childlike wonder' (Noonan 2013). Indeed, research by Ashton (2013a) with teacher practitioners articulated the importance of exploring with students the challenges they would face in industry. Along these lines, raising the challenges of working in the creative industries opens up a space for students to consider 'not becoming' creative workers (see Gill and Pratt 2008). This scenario, in which students from creative courses reassess working in the creative industries, might be usefully contrasted with those graduating from courses that are less obviously linked, through course content and accreditation, to the creative industries. This seems especially important if the higher education experience of these students covers less the kinds of critical interventions that might be possible within creative courses (Ashton 2013a, 2013b).

Degrees of relevance

In their analysis of data collected by the Higher Education Statistical Agency on the employment trends and patterns of 'bohemian' graduates, Comunian, Faggian and Jewell suggest that, '[…] the creative skills of graduates in these disciplines are not fully valued and appreciated in the job market (both in creative and non-creative occupations)' (2011, 305). This analysis resonates with approaches to embedded creative work in referencing how the skills of creative students may be relevant in creative and non-creative occupations. It does, however, also raise the issue of students from creative courses being unemployable in both.

Being unable to fulfil creative work career aspirations leads to the kinds of temporary circumstances and unclear pathways that the formulations raised in this article seek to highlight. The distance between student aspirations and graduation circumstances bring to the surface the obstacles, barriers and challenges that education for creative work must address. Ball, Pollard, and Stanley note that the graduates surveyed in their project 'overwhelmingly aspired to creative careers', and that 'their specific goals aligned with their subject discipline' (2010, xxiv). Alignment though can be less than straightforward. For example, Guile argues that, 'although academic and vocational programmes of study at any level can provide a grounding and inspiration for learners, they are unlikely to provide the conditions to develop vocational practice' (2009, 774). These comments open up the possibility for addressing unexpected pathways, not only in terms of students on non-creative courses that go on to work in non-creative occupations in the creative industries, but also students on non-creative courses that go on to work in creative occupations in the creative industries. In other words, within the context of transferable skills, what are the distinctive aspects of degree courses linked to the creative industries for working in creative occupations?

In comments that echo with Ball, Pollard, and Stanley's (2010) findings on the desire for students to pursue their creative career aspirations, McRobbie (2011) suggests that for those trained in the arts and cultural and humanities fields, having an interesting creative job is part of their social identity. On this basis, being unable to develop a career within the specialist or embedded mode of creative work may be of concern for students and graduates. McRobbie's (2011) argument, however, goes on to question the extent to which not securing creative work should be seen as a 'failure to live up to the dream of the talent-led economy'. For those attentive to the challenges of working in the creative industries, such as elaborated on in academic literature (Gill and Pratt 2008; Oakley 2008; Hesmondhalgh and Baker 2011) and linked explicitly to higher education (Ashton 2011c; Ashton and Noonan 2013), a movement away from working in the creative industries could be a career strategy or choice. For those whose degree course, either through work placements or other forms of curriculum content, provides less in-depth and/or cautionary insights, the uncompromised allure of the creative industries may be strong.

In this scenario, students from a range of different degree backgrounds are able to pursue creative careers and, within a labour market characterised by oversupply (Oakley 2013), there are ramifications for students on creative courses. In terms of employer preferences, Ashton (2010) has addressed how 'traditional' degrees, such as art and physics, were preferred by games industry employers compared to newer degrees that might be more explicitly industry focused, such as games design and games programming. The standing of certain degrees and the extent to which established degree subjects or certain universities and university courses are preferred were evident here. The acquisition and demonstration of relevant and desirable employability attributes for creative work that can come from degree courses that are not vocationally explicit can include social capital and networking (Lee 2013) and access to internships (Zelenko and Bridgstock 2014). A further perspective focusing on the entrepreneurial and training possibilities gained outside of a degree programme through student media and union activities is indicated by Long (2011). It is clear that pathways from higher education into the creative industries and creative employment are not limited by disciplinary boundaries. As such, the boundaries and margins of creative work can be further opened up and the possibilities for understanding secure pathways and expected trajectories further negotiated.

Conclusion

This article has addressed the complexities of creative work through emphasising varied creative career pathways and the tensions and negotiations around securing creative work employment. The Creative Trident approach extends analysis of creative work opportunities and practices beyond working in a specialist mode within the creative industries. Further extending the survey of how and where creative work takes place can reveal temporary, unstable and transient forms of work, in which movements in, out and alongside creative employment are common. This article has signalled a range of factors that can shape and often impede opportunities for securing creative work for those who would identify as creative workers, and for those seeking to establish their creative worker biographies upon graduation.

This discussion of 'non-creative' workers and the margins of creative work could be further developed with reference to Negus' (2002) discussion of cultural intermediaries and Mayer's (2011) study of the invisible labour of television set factory labourers.

The specific themes employed in parts three and four to survey existing research and literature show some common circumstances and challenges faced by established and emerging creative workers. In signalling the diverse arrangements and scenarios in which creative workers are (un)able to undertake creative employment, this article is only a starting point that encourages further empirical investigation. Echoing Gill and Pratt's (2008) comments on potential non-becomings, the question of wanting to, but not being able to, secure creative work should animate any analysis of how creative work figures within the economy at large. With regard to higher education and professional development for creative workers, this article points to an even greater range of creative worker identity positions and career circumstances. Recognising the specificity of specialist and embedded modes of creative work ensures understanding of different professional identities, career trajectories and occupational cultures. The temporary and contingent nature of categorisation within these modes is apparent though. In this respect, understanding creative education and creative work can be as much about understanding broader and more general overlaps and intersections with education and work.

References

Allen, K., J. Quinn, S. Hollingworth, and A. Rose. 2012. "Becoming Employable Students and 'Ideal' Creative Workers: Exclusion and Inequality in Higher Education Work Placements." *British Journal of Sociology of Education* 34 (3): 431–452.

Ashton, D. 2010. "Productive Passions and Everyday Pedagogies: Exploring the Industry-ready Agenda in Higher Education." *Art, Design and Communication in Higher Education* 9 (1): 41–56.

Ashton, D. 2011a. "Pathways to Creativity: Self-Learning and Customising in/for the Creative Economy." *Journal of Cultural Economy* 4 (2): 189–203.

Ashton, D. 2011c. "Media Work and the Creative Industries: Identity Work." *Education and Training* 53 (6): 546–560.

Ashton, D. 2013a. "Industry Practitioners in Higher Education: Values, Identities and Cultural Work." In *Cultural Work and Higher Education*, edited by D. Ashton, and C. Noonan, 172–192. Basingstoke: Palgrave Macmillan.

Ashton, D. 2013b. "Cultural Workers in-the-Making." *European Journal of Cultural Studies* 16 (4): 468–488.

Ashton, D., and N. Noonan. 2013. *Cultural Work and Higher Education*. Basingstoke: Palgrave Macmillan.

Bakhshi, H., A. Freeman, and P. Higgs. 2012. *A Dynamic Mapping of the UK's Creative Economy*. London: NESTA.

Ball, L., E. Pollard, and N. Stanley. 2010. *Creative Graduates Creative Futures*. London: Institute for Employment Studies.

Banks, M., and D. Hesmondhalgh. 2009. "Looking for Work in Creative Industries Policy." *International Journal of Cultural Policy* 15 (4): 415–430.

Bennett, D. 2009. "Academy and the Real World: Developing Realistic Notions of Career in the Performing Arts." *Arts & Humanities in Higher Education* 8 (3): 309–327.

Berger, R., J. Wardle, and M. Zezulkova. 2013. "No Longer Just Making Tea: Media Work Placements and Work-Based Learning in Higher Education." In *Cultural Work and Higher Education*, edited by D. Ashton, and C. Noonan, 87–109. Basingstoke: Palgrave Macmillan.

Blair, H. 2002. "You're Only as Good as Your Last Job: The Labour Process and Labour Market in the British Film Industry." *Work, Employment & Society* 15 (1): 149–169.

Bridgstock, R. 2005. "Australian Artists, Starving and Well-nourished: What Can we Learn from the Prototypical Protean Career?" *Australian Journal of Career Development* 14 (3): 40–47.

Bridgstock, R. 2011. "Making It Creatively: Building Sustainable Careers in the Arts and Creative Industries." *Australian Career Practitioner Magazine* 22 (2): 11–13.

Brown, P., A. Hesketh, and S. Williams. 2003. "Employability in a Knowledge-driven Economy." *Journal of Education And Work* 16 (2): 107–126.

Carrot Workers Collective. 2011. *Surviving Internships: A Counter Guide to Free Labour in the Arts*. London.

CCI (Centre of Excellence for Creative Industries and Innovation). n.d. Skills and Creative Capital. Accessed May 13, 2013. http://www.cci.edu.au/research.

Comunian, R., A. Faggian, and S. Jewell. 2011. "Winning and Losing in the Creative Industries: An Analysis of Creative Graduate's Career Opportunities across Creative Disciplines." *Cultural Trends* 20 (3–4): 291–308.

Creative and Cultural Skills. 2008. *Creative and Cultural Industry: Impact and Footprints 08–09*. London: Creative and Cultural Skills.

Creative Skillset. 2009. *Strategic Skills Assessment for the Creative Media Industry*. Accessed July 5, 2012. http://www.creativeskillset.org/uploads/pdf/asset_14582.pdf.

Creative Skillset. n.d. 'Research'. Accessed May 13, 2013. http://www.creativeskillset.org/research/article_6916_1.asp.

Creech, A., I. Papageorgi, C. Duffy, F. Morton, E. Haddon, J. Potter, C. de Bezenac, T. Whyton, E. Himonides, and G. Welch. 2008. "From Music Student to Professional: The Process of Transition." *British Journal of Music Education* 25 (03): 315–331.

Cunningham, S. 2011. "Developments in Measuring the "Creative" Workforce." *Cultural Trends* 20 (1): 25–40.

Cunningham, S. 2013. *Hidden Innovation*. St Lucia: University of Queensland Press.

DCMS (Department of Culture, Media and Sport). 2001. *Creative Industries Mapping Document*. London: HMSO.

DCMS (Department of Culture, Media and Sport). 2008. *Creative Britain*. London: HMSO.

Flew, T. 2012. *The Creative Industries*. London: SAGE.

Gill, R., and A. Pratt. 2008. "In the Social Factory? Immaterial Labour, Precariousness and Cultural Work." *Theory, Culture & Society* 25 (1): 1–30.

Grugulis, I., and D. Stoyanova. 2011. "The Missing Middle: Communities of Practice in a Freelance Labour Market." *Work, Employment & Society* 25 (2): 342–351.

Guile, D. 2009. "Conceptualizing the Transition from Education to Work as Vocational Practice: Lessons from the UK's Creative and Cultural Sector." *British Educational Research Journal* 35 (5): 761–779.

Guile, D. 2010. "Learning to Work in the Creative and Cultural Sector: New Spaces, Pedagogies and Expertise." *Journal of Education Policy* 25 (4): 465–484.

Hartley, J., J. Potts, S. Cunningham, T. Flew, M. Keane, and J. Banks. 2013. *Key Concepts in Creative Industries*. London: SAGE.

Haukka, S. 2010. "Education-to-work Transitions of Aspiring Creatives." *Cultural Trends* 20 (1): 41–64.

Hearn, G., and R. Bridgstock. 2014. "The Curious Case of the Embedded Creative: Creative Cultural Occupations outside the Creative Industries." In *The Handbook of Management and Creativity*, edited by C. Bilton, and S. Cummings, 39–56. Cheltenham: Edward Elgar.

Hesmondhalgh, D., and S. Baker. 2011. *Creative Labour: Media Work in Three Cultural Industries*. London: Routledge.

Higgs, P., and S. Cunningham. 2008. "Embedded Creatives – Revealing the Extent and Contribution of Creative Professionals Working throughout the Economy." Paper presented at International Forum on the Creative Economy, Quebec, March 17–18.

Higgs, P., S. Cunningham, and H. Bakhshi. 2008. *Beyond the Creative Industries: Mapping the Creative Economy in the United Kingdom*. London: NESTA.

Higher Education Funding Council for England. (n.d.) "What We Do – Learning and Teaching in Higher Education." [Online]. Accessed November 6, 2012. https://www.hefce.ac.uk/whatwedo/lt/.

Lee, D. 2011. "Networks, Cultural Capital and Creative Labour in the British Independent Television Industry." *Media, Culture and Society* 33 (4): 549–565.

Lee, D. 2013. "Creative Networks and Social Capital." In *Cultural Work and Higher Education*, edited by D. Ashton, and C. Noonan, 195–213. Basingstoke: Palgrave Macmillan.

Long, P. 2011. "Student Music." *Art Marketing: An International Journal* 1 (2): 121–135.

Marsden, D. 2007. "Labour Market Segmentation in Britain: The Decline of Occupational Labour Markets and the Spread of Entry Tournaments." *Economies et Societés* 28: 963–998.

Mayer, V. 2011. *Below the Line: Producers and Production Studies in the New Television Economy*. London: Duke University Press.

McGuigan, J. 2009. *Cool Capitalism*. Cambridge: Pluto Press.

McRobbie, A. 2002. "Clubs to Companies: Notes on the Decline of Political Culture in Speeded Up Creative Worlds." *Cultural Studies* 16 (4): 516–531.

McRobbie, A. 2011. "Re-thinking Creative Economy as Radical Social Enterprise." *Variant* 41: 32–33.

Neff, G., E. Wissinger, and S. Zukin. 2005. "Entrepreneurial Labor among Cultural Producers: "Cool" Jobs in "Hot" Industries." *Social Semiotics* 15 (3): 307–334.

Negus, K. 2002. "The Work of Cultural Intermediaries and the Enduring Distance Between Production and Consumption." *Cultural Studies* 16 (4): 501–515.

Negus, K. 2006. "Rethinking Creative Production Away from the Cultural Industries." In *Media and Cultural Theory*, edited by J. Curran, and D. Morley, 197–208. London: Routledge.

Nixon, S., and B. Crewe. 2004. "Pleasure at Work? Gender, Consumption and Work-based Identities in the Creative Industries." *Consumption, Markets and Culture* 7 (2): 129–147.

Noonan, C. 2013. "Smashing Childlike Wonder? The Early Journey into Higher Education." In *Cultural Work and Higher Education*, edited by D. Ashton, and C. Noonan, 133–153. Basingstoke: Palgrave Macmillan.

Oakley, K. 2009/2008. *'Art Works' – Cultural Labour Markets: A Literature Review.* London: Creativity, Culture and Education.

Oakley, K. 2013. "Making Workers. Higher Education and the Cultural Industries Workplace." In *Cultural Work and Higher Education*, edited by D. Ashton, and C. Noonan, 25–44. Basingstoke: Palgrave Macmillan.

Pollard, E. 2013. "Making Your Way. Empirical Evidence from a Survey of 3,500 Graduates." In *Cultural Work and Higher Education*, edited by D. Ashton, and C. Noonan, 45–66. Basingstoke: Palgrave Macmillan.

Potts, J. D., and S. Cunningham. 2008. "Four Models of the Creative Industries." *International Journal of Cultural Policy* 14 (3): 233–247.

Saha, A. 2013. "The Cultural Industries in a Critical Multicultural Pedagogy." In *Cultural Work and Higher Education*, edited by D. Ashton, and C. Noonan, 214–231. Basingstoke: Palgrave Macmillan.

Stoyanova, D., and I. Grugulis. 2012. "Tournament Careers: Working in UK Television." In *Careers in Creative Industries*, edited by C. Mathieu, 88–106. London: Routledge.

Taylor, S., and K. Littleton. 2012. *Contemporary Identities of Creativity and Creative Work.* Farnham: Ashgate.

Throsby, D., and A. Zednik. 2011. "Multiple Job-holding and Artistic Careers: Some Empirical Evidence." *Cultural Trends* 20 (1): 9–24.

Tomlinson, M. 2007. "Graduate Employability and Student Attitudes and Orientations to the Labour Market." *Journal of Education and Work* 20 (4): 285–304.

Universities UK. 2010a. *Creating Prosperity: The Role of Higher Education in Driving the UK's Creative Economy.* London: Universities UK.

Universities UK. 2010b. *Patterns of Higher Education Institutions in the UK Tenth report.* Accessed November 14, 2012. http://www.universitiesuk.ac.uk/Publications/Documents/PatternsOfHigherEducationInstitutionsInTheUK.pdf.

Zelenko, O., and R. Bridgstock. 2014. "Developing Agency in the Creative Career: A Design-based Framework for Work Integrated Learning." In *Creative Work beyond the Creative Industries: Innovation, Employment, and Education*, edited by G. Hearn, B. Goldsmith, R. Bridgstock, and J. Rodgers, 211–225. Cheltenham: Edward Elgar Publishing.

The careers of fine artists and the embedded creative

Charlotte Carey

Department of Strategy, Economics and Marketing, Birmingham City Business School, Birmingham City University, Birmingham, UK

While there is a growing body of scholarship on the creative industries and on the career trajectories of graduates from creative industries programmes, there has to date only been a limited amount of research that examines in detail, the careers of fine arts graduates. Fine art is arguably the least 'vocational' of creative disciplines, in that there are relatively few employers that seek to employ fine artists as fine artists. If fine arts graduates are not employed in their chosen field – that is, in the 'Creative Trident' terminology, in a core creative occupation – how do their careers parallel or differ from those of other creative graduates? Do they find employment as 'embedded creatives', using or applying their experience and practice in sectors beyond the core creative industries, or as 'support workers', enabling and facilitating the creative work of others? Do they experience portfolio careers? And how do their artistic training and attitudes to creativity affect their working relationships and experiences? This article draws on rich qualitative data about the experiences of a small group of graduates (including the author) who all graduated from the same course at the same institution in the UK in 1994, to provide some insights into the career paths and trajectories of a sample of fine arts graduates.

Introduction

Across the creative industries, 'most creative [firms] start small, based on one or two people playing multiple roles' (Bilton 2006, 27). Artists, however, arguably behave differently. An artist's career is shaped, to an extent, by their ability to market themselves. Menger (1999) suggests that the ability to build a public persona is important to an artist's career trajectory, in terms of acquiring and sustaining recognition for their talent. This can often be at odds with the underlying motivation of an artist where they are often driven by their artistic pursuit over any commercial imperative (Kubacki and Croft 2011). These motivations and drivers are explored in detail by Bridgstock (2013) who identifies, for example, key differences between artist entrepreneurs and general entrepreneurs:

> Arts has characteristics which distinguish it from entrepreneurship in other sectors, including contextual and sectoral features, the nature and processes of artistic work, the kinds of value that artistic work can add, and the motivations of the artist. Entrepreneurs in other fields are often 'pulled' to becoming entrepreneurial, driven by the challenge of starting a new venture or developing a new product. By contrast, artists are often 'pushed' to entrepreneurship through necessity. (124)

Whether artists share characteristics with other creative disciplines is discussed elsewhere. For example, while they tend to work on an individual basis, there appears to still be a high level of networking in terms of sharing and collaborating on exhibiting opportunities (Bridgstock 2005).

Other issues have also been identified; for example, there are differences in terms of gender and artist careers, with female artists struggling to establish themselves and experiencing greater disruption and breaks within their careers (Brooks and Daniluk 1998). However, recent research suggests that potentially female artists, particularly female artists who are parents, experience something of a renaissance of their artistic output during middle age (Carey 2013). More generally artists' careers are characterised by needing to balance a combination of types of work in terms of their artistic work, paid creative and paid non-creative work (Throsby 2007). Linked to all of this is work which seeks to establish the part that fine artists play more widely within the world of work, acknowledging that they frequently require work outside of their training. As Oakley, Sperry, and Pratt (2008) discuss when considering the impact of fine artists' on innovation, more widely:

> from an innovation perspective, the importance of this form of work organisation is perhaps less what it tells us about the labour market and more what it tells us about the crossover and cross-fertilisation of people and ideas across the arts and between the arts and non-arts worlds. (Oakley, Sperry, and Pratt 2008, 6)

The creative entrepreneur has been identified as one who has the 'creativity to unlock the wealth that lies within themselves' (Howkins 2001, 128) suggesting that creative individuals might need only their intellectual capital to start an enterprise. The relationship between entrepreneurship and the creative industries is explored in *Entrepreneurship in the Creative Industries; an International Perspective* (Henry and de Bruin 2008). Here, further definitions of the creative entrepreneur are provided; for example, the 'Art–entrepreneur' is suggested to be someone who is a 'holder of tacit knowledge that is realised as part of human capital and includes individual skill, competence, commitment and creativity-based mindsets' (Aggestam 2008, 30). While the literature related to the creative industries has focussed heavily on the entrepreneurial contribution these individuals make, recent research questions the rationale for imposing this entrepreneurial discourse onto the fine artist (Carey 2013).

Other research explores when and how enterprise and entrepreneurship are taught to 'creatives' (Carey and Naudin 2006), by looking for links between existing pedagogies within schools of art and design and the arguably entrepreneurial outcomes (Carey and Matlay 2007, 2010; Penaluna and Penaluna 2009). What has emerged offers reasonable insight into how this education might influence careers within the sector. For example, Carey and Matlay (2007) discuss 'implicit enterprise education', which refers to those aspects built into the teaching methods that potentially lead to entrepreneurial outcomes: 'lecturers who are practitioners, the use of experiential learning, responding to real-life projects, the "crit" (for assessment) and the degree show' (440).

Given the gaps in the research about the individual and lived experiences of fine arts graduates who emerge into a highly competitive industry without clear vocational opportunities, this article uses interviews to explore the career trajectories of a cohort of fine arts graduates. This research adds to a body of largely quantitative, survey tracking-based work that provides high level generalisable findings about graduates across universities and many disciplines, such as *Creative Graduates, Creative Futures* (Ball, Pollard, and Stanley 2010), and observational and theoretical work around fine arts curricula and university engagement with creative entrepreneurship (Carey and Matlay 2007, 2010; Penaluna and Penaluna 2009).

Method

This study captures the career stories of a cohort of fine arts graduates, through a series of one-to-one semistructured and retrospective interviews. These took place some 18 years after graduation and 21 years after the commencement of their fine art course, giving plenty of time for the cohort to try out and settle in to their careers and become established in one or more occupations. The sample group – which includes the author of this study – had all graduated from the same course in the same year. Fine art was chosen as potentially the least vocational of the creative disciplines (Oakley, Sperry, and Pratt 2008), in terms of numbers of jobs adverts actively seeking fine arts graduates to act as artists. The assumption was then that they would be 'pushed' into entrepreneurship; Higgs, Cunningham, and Bakshi (2008) suggest that some 92% of artists are self-employed, or working outside of their original creative discipline. Another recent survey suggested that self-employment amongst artists (72%) was considerably higher than for the creative industries as a whole (41%) (Jones 2011, 2).

The timing of the study and access to the sample group was also important. These individuals had graduated in 1994. This was three years before the term the 'creative industries' had emerged, meaning this group would have worked through the various UK local and national government policies for supporting the creative industries, initiated by the then Labour administration. Importantly, the group was at an age where they were 'at a point in their lives where personal responsibilities might have had an influence over their careers, e.g. parenthood, home ownership or other caring responsibilities' (Carey 2013, 73). The sample offered a concentrated group, all of whom had had the same starting point, which offered insight into how their creativity had developed and where it ended up taking them. The author's own position and insider perspective offers additional insight and a shortcut to understanding some of the experience of the participants. Following a prolonged period of time pursuing the group, the eventual sample of those interviewed was eight women and five men, representing 22% of the original graduating cohort.

The next sections discuss the results aiming to answer questions such as: How did these fine artists fare within the jobs market? How useful was their fine art degree? Did their training have any bearing on how they were perceived within the workplace and how did they perceive themselves? And how were they perceived because of their art school training?

Fine artists in the workplace

This section provides an overview of the types of careers that participants experienced, followed by an exploration of the effects of a fine art education in terms of how this cohort's creative skills impacted on their sometimes 'non-creative' careers. Finally, the participants' sense of themselves is discussed, in terms of their own artistic and career identity and entrepreneurial outcomes.

Participants' careers

Following a brief spell of working as an artist, including living and working in an artists' community, where she continued to make and exhibit work, participant 1 trained as an art therapist. Throughout this period, she continued to make and exhibit her own work. This training led to a career working as a senior art psycho-therapist (currently on a part-time basis). Throughout this period, she has continued to pursue her own practice as an artist with ongoing attempts to exhibit and sell work. In addition to this, she has had a significant parenting role that has impacted the time she spends in paid employment.

Working now as a senior lecturer within a school of art and design, participant 2 is, in addition to his lecturing role, an active art maker. He describes this: 'if I was to sum it up in terms of what I am as a practitioner, I'm a creative director, which was pointed out to me by one of my senior colleagues about five years ago.' His career has evolved from an initial split of working as a practising artist and doing non-creative work (e.g. bar work) to sustain his practice, moving within a couple of years to a design and management role working within a small graphic and web design company to his existing role, teaching and managing design courses. Throughout this time, he has continued to make and exhibit work.

Participant 3 left her artistic practice relatively early and concentrated on working within health care and roles within care homes. This led to retraining as an art therapist. She has for the majority of her career worked as an art psycho-therapist. In addition to this, she has a significant parenting role that has impacted the time she spends in paid employment. She has ongoing aspirations of picking up her arts practice, but has made no attempt to develop this.

Like most of the others in the cohort, participant 4 started out her career hoping to work predominantly as an artist. This led to a succession of jobs loosely connected to the creative industries sector, but frequently administrative in nature. Finally, when the struggle to source employment which would be creatively fulfilling seemed unachievable, and she was unable to tolerate working any longer in roles that were not satisfying to her, she trained to become a school teacher. She works part-time as an art teacher in secondary school, 'as my Head of Art says, she uses all her creativity inspiring the kids to do their final, you know, get their pieces together and final work together.' While this indicates how her fine art practice is embedded in her working life, she also maintains her arts practice and has had ongoing exhibiting opportunities and makes a small income from sales. Additionally, she has a significant parenting role that has effected the time she spends in paid employment.

Following a number of years working in various roles within the arts, participant 5 has spent the majority of the period since graduating as a full-time parent. Throughout this period, she harboured an intense desire to continue her creative practice. However, this is not to suggest that she has felt bereft of creative output as her relationship with creativity evolved: 'when I was at home with the kids, I realised that creativity was lots of things and lots of, you know, it was cooking a meal and it was making some marmalade.' At the time of writing, this has manifested as a refocusing of her career. Having gone back to university and studied illustration, she is now working as a freelance illustrator and artist and works on paid commissions.

On completing her degree, participant 6 went back home to her family. She took retail jobs to pay her way and soon stopped making art. She did, however, take on some voluntary work within a notable art gallery. This led to a new direction:

> it gave me a real insight into how galleries worked and how creative the process is of my working with artists so that kind of took me on a different trajectory. … I was still naïve as to what curating was as a practice. … I

> moved to London and started managing to get work in gallery spaces, but still doing voluntary work, which led to curator roles, eventually.

Several jobs and moves around the country and she now works as the director and curator at a small but notable art gallery in the United Kingdom.

Participant 7 is a design and technology technician in a secondary school. He has been working in this occupation for approximately 12 years. In addition to this, he makes and designs bespoke pieces of furniture. Soon after he graduated, he went to live and work in an artist community. Here, young artists worked and exhibited and attempted to forge their careers. After a couple of years, the community broke up and the buildings were demolished. What followed was several years of freelance work, commissions, set design and finally, having moved around the country, he moved to London where, having spent a year working in a record shop and having a break from the pursuit of creative work, he then participated in a furniture design course. Not long after that he was appointed in his current role. Initially, this was viewed as an opportunity to have paid access to a workshop, but subsequently, his view has evolved: 'I never thought I'd be there for 10 years, but 10 years later, I'm still there and it's now a full-time job and I do enjoy it, I mean, I've discovered that I really enjoy working with students, young people.' He continues to pursue and make a small income from his own work.

Participant 8's career began like many others with a variety of creative activities. He remained in Wolverhampton, producing small urban street art, working on visuals for night clubs and collaborating with other recent graduates. This led to some sound work and a brief career as a musician creating electronic music and a move to London. Following some managerial and creative differences, he ended his music career and spent a number of years working in a succession of non-creative jobs feeling unfulfilled creatively. A number of chance encounters and a confident and creative application form led him to a coveted BBC traineeship. Working as a 'creative' (formerly referred to as a 'promo' producer), he was quickly promoted and has built a career working for a number of well-known British TV companies and channels in a full-time capacity in this role.

Participant 9 works as a buildings manager. She left art school with the intention of pursuing a career as an artist. This led to a move to London, where she spent a number of years attempting to 'break into the London arts scene' and was a recipient of a number of government funding initiatives. During this time, she also took paid work as a health and safety advisor, where her employers paid for her to be trained; this led to a Master's degree and an eventual career change. She has not been a practicing artist for the last 15 years and instead has concentrated on building her career in buildings management. She has subsequently left the United Kingdom and has recently been involved in the design and build of new 'eco-buildings'.

Participant 9 is one of the three participants who no longer consider themselves to be explicitly working within the creative industries. However, she still identifies herself as creative within her career.

Participant 10 moved back home to London following completion of his degree. Quite soon after graduating, he sought employment due to financial necessity. Initially, he found work as a photocopy technician and later as a digital print technician. This has developed into his career. In terms of his creative output, he has continued to make art and pursued a writing ambition despite not attempting to exhibit or sell his work. He views his work as a print technician as an opportunity to be creative 'there is a creative aspect to it, so at least I've got that and you know, it's quite important, 'cause I did the office job and it just bored me to hell, nice company but I have to be doing something creative, otherwise I'll go spare.'

Participant 11's career began with a flourish of activity including a Fine Art MA and a fair amount of travelling, creating and exhibiting throughout, her work making use of photography. However, within a couple of years, the need to make money led her to taking a role within a local newspaper as a photographer. While there she was able to exercise her writing skills, was quickly promoted and within six months had moved to London and was working for a national newspaper as a journalist. She continued writing, both as a journalist and travel writer for 10 years before chronic illness led to a career break. While recovering she left London and resumed her artistic career and now works as a full-time artist and freelance writer away from the somewhat cut-throat environment of the newspaper industry.

Following her first degree, participant 12 undertook teacher training; however, not long after she graduated, she decided that 'teaching was not the right career path.' Due to family commitments, she needed to be geographically located in a particular area and took on a succession of short-term jobs. A number of years passed and eventually she took an entirely different career route. Responding to a newspaper advert, she made her way into 'business banking'. Like other female participants when she started her family, having begun to build her career in banking, she started to work part-time and caring commitments became her main priority. It is with some regret that she highlights that 'I have not even pursued it [art] as a hobby.'

Following a brief spell of moving back to his family and working in bar jobs, Participant 13 enjoyed a successful career working as a freelance and microbusiness owner/manager in London for over 15 years. Here, his work was as a creative within a creative companies working as a special effects artist within the design and media fields. A desire for a different kind of lifestyle for himself and his growing family led him to emigrate outside of the United Kingdom where he now runs a small business outside of the creative industries.

Types of careers

Broadly speaking, the careers of the participants fall into the three main types of creative work: 'specialist' creatives, including creative workers in creative industries; 'support' staff in those industries providing management, secretarial, administrative or accountancy backup; and creative individuals 'embedded' in other industries not defined as 'creative' (Higgs, Cunningham, and Bakshi 2008, 3). The majority of participants in this study (10 of 13) were working in what could broadly be described as creative roles. This was split between those who were arguably 'embedded' outside the creative industries and those who were 'specialists' within creative organisations.

It is worth taking a moment to provide a distinction here. These categories are in some ways problematic for fine artists. For example, two of the participants were working as art psycho-therapists. In these roles, it could be argued they were 'applying' their arts practice in a similar way to those who worked as art teachers, but neither of these occupations is classified as creative according to Higgs, Cunningham, and Bakshi (2008) definition of creative workers. It is important to note that they were 'applying' their arts practice as opposed to 'practicing their own arts practice'; they were applying creative cultural expertise to an output other than art and thus did not fall into the Trident categorisation of creative workers. However, they might be seen as 'embedded creatives' in a broader definition of the term, as they were employed doing creative work in organisations outside the creative industries.

For the majority of participants, it could also be argued that there was an element of 'portfolio' work, in that they were, on the one hand, employed and to a greater or lesser degree applying their fine art training, and, on the other hand, they remained practising artists outside of formal employment. There were, for the majority, ongoing attempts to make, exhibit and sell their own art work, often on a self-employment basis. As established by Throsby (2007), artists frequently undertake one arts-related employment activity to financially service another. Two participants managed to make art as their central activity and means of making a living. However, there remained blurring of employment type boundaries and crossovers, as well as a lot of movement between arts employment undertaken. Throsby (2007) highlighted 'three alternatives: creative work, arts-related work and non-arts work' (395); this definition would seem to fit slightly more comfortably with this group than strict Creative Trident classifications of creative vs non-creative. What also became evident was that even those who identified themselves as those not working within either a creative organisation or carrying out a creative role appeared to be behaving creatively and, in some instances, attributed this to their fine art education.

The careers of artists are frequently piecemeal, in that they may be managing a number of roles at a given time, frequently using paid 'other' work to subsidise their arts work (Throsby 2007). The experience of the cohort studied here bears out this finding. Although it is somewhat beyond the scope of this study, there was evidence that some members of the study group experienced a protean career (where the emphasis and direction of the career sits with the individual as opposed to an organisation [Bridgstock 2005]). There was a tendency, particularly amongst the female participants, to be working on a number of projects at the same time, including some paid work and unpaid carer or family responsibilities. While often precarious, another potential advantage to portfolio careers is the flexibility they allow. This means employment can be tailored alongside other interests or priorities.

Art school education

Previous research suggests that one way of measuring the impact of the fine art degree can be measured in terms of a fine artist's contribution to innovation, in the sense that there is a 'crossover' or cross pollination from their creative work to their non-creative work (Oakley, Sperry, and Pratt 2008). This was evident in this study when participants engaged in multiple concurrent roles, who tended to express their ability to approach 'non-creative' tasks more creatively, to be more concerned with aesthetics than their 'non-artist' colleagues and to be able to manage their time well. Interestingly, this extended beyond the creative work activities. As one participant identified, the self-discipline required in fine art education, which is frequently characterised by self-directed pedagogies, was a useful precursor to a life of project management. These types of skills have been identified elsewhere in discussion surrounding the potential impact of art and design education on the development of entrepreneurial attributes (Carey and Matlay 2007). These findings suggest that there may be unanticipated benefits of some of the 'implicit' enterprise pedagogies within art and design education: they imply that the use of the 'crit', practitioners as lecturers, project-based work and student managed workloads, amongst others (Carey and Naudin 2006; Carey and Matlay 2007, 2010; Penaluna and Penaluna 2009) have the potential to develop business skills amongst artists.

The interviews with the cohort provided some evidence to suggest that skills developed through fine art training were manifesting within the participants' work lives. Although participants felt to an extent ill-prepared for life beyond university – for example, they had not been provided with any 'explicit' enterprise or entrepreneurship education – there was a suggestion that other benefits and entrepreneurial outcomes, characteristics and traits had accrued from their fine art course:

> People that have done fine art they are self-disciplined and they drive themselves, but that doesn't always connect that you can be self-disciplined and drive your own practice, but the marketing of your practice is a separate thing and reaching the people you want to reach and understanding your practice enough to be able to break it down, it's like a different skill. (Participant 5)

This suggests that the practice and self-led nature of the courses equip graduates with the discipline required, but the practical business skills associated with running a business, for example marketing and financial accounting skills, were missing. However, it also indicates that as employees these individuals might be able to apply this self-discipline within an organisational setting:

> I suppose being at art school, you become more aware of design and promotion. (Participant 7)

This participant highlights the development of the individual's design literacy and, it could be argued, how design is used within a marketing context:

> In a funny kind of way it gave me a great sense of time-management and allowed me to think creatively about all kinds of things not just art. Studying art gives you the ability to have a creative perspective on most things. It's given me the confidence also to try new things, which inevitably has led me to where I am now. (Participant 13)

Interestingly, this final participant, a serial entrepreneur both in creative and non-creative enterprises, credits his fine art education with equipping him with business skills in terms of time management, but also offering him a creative outlook and the confidence to try other career options.

While explicit enterprise education was lacking for these participants, there is some evidence to suggest that the existing methods of teaching fine art may well lend themselves to implicit enterprise education and to the development of entrepreneurial traits. And yet without explicit business skills being taught, upon graduating some students were unable, and perhaps to some extent unwilling, to fully exploit their talent for economic gain.

The fine art training of the participants did impact on how they perceived themselves and also how their colleagues perceived them in the work place:

> I feel like it's gone through waves, you know, I've been doing my degree when I thought, oh this is really my identity as somebody who makes art or whatever. (Participant 1)

> I still feel that I'm still practising, but not making work. (Participant 6)

> I realised I'm completely mental, because I hadn't done any work for, what, 10, 15 years and I still pictured myself as an artist. (Participant 5)

> It is strange but I was thinking of it this morning 'cause I thought about what I was going to say and I guessed you'd say, well, what is your job and I thought, well, straight away I said technician in my mind, then I thought, oh actually, I am but honestly, I don't see that as my full thing, I am, don't know

> what you call it, but like a sort of the furniture maker as well, you know, even though I don't get loads of, well, hardly any money from it. Mentally, it's still part of my job, I'm still trying to push it. (Participant 7)

What is evident is that the participants of the study have retained a strong sense of themselves as artists and have a desire to create. There appear to be many factors that inform this apart from satisfying their human need (Pratt 2004), although their compulsion to create clearly helped to reinforce their artistic identity and their continued sense of presence within the art world. Interestingly, this was still the case in some instances for those who have not been actively involved in making art for a number of years. Their training appeared to have had other legacies in terms of how they were perceived by others as well as how they approached tasks:

> Everyone called me 'art teacher' in the news room, because I'd come in ... I even dressed artily and of course ... Canary Wharf, people don't dress like that, they're all in black pinstripe suits and I was arty, I suppose, so they called me 'art teacher' and so, it really felt that somehow I didn't belong, but maybe my brain belonged there, but the rest of me didn't. (Participant 11)

> I have to do a lot of project management and when doing so feel like the design process and creativity are really drawn upon. (Participant 9)

Generally speaking, the participants' views of creativity expanded as their own careers took on broader remits. A somewhat negative assessment of their expanding views of creativity would be to suggest that this was a convenient adaption to sustain their ongoing sense of self as a creative individual. These last two extracts (one from a buildings manager and one from a journalist) highlight the ongoing importance of the 'creative self' to the participants and the impact of this ongoing creative identity on how participants engage with others, how they are received by others, and the ways they undertake their 'non-creative' work (as defined by Throsby 2007).

The careers of the participants went through periods of feast and famine in terms of their own personal creative work, which may be considered reflective of the well-established tension within the careers of artists and other creative individuals between art and commerce (Throsby 2007). Within this, there appeared to be both push and pull factors contributing to entrepreneurial activity. For example, push factors manifested when participants felt that the only way that they would be able to carry on with their artistic practice, which they craved, was by adopting entrepreneurial options/behaviours. Similarly, pull factors emerged when participants saw that entrepreneurship offered them the freedom to create. Amongst all of this, there were additional tensions. There were practical considerations, such as how to go about selling one's own work? This led to the identification of a number of different values that participants associated with their work, which made selling and marketing problematic. These included the following: aesthetic, financial and emotional values and the inter-relationship of the three presented blocks to entrepreneurial activity. This insight appears to confirm Bridgstock's observation that artists are often 'pushed' into entrepreneurship out of necessity, rather than choosing an entrepreneurial path (Bridgstock 2013, 127). Entrepreneurial activity, in terms of being an artist, was seldom a deliberate attempt to build a business and was more often an outcome (the participant who was a serial entrepreneur created businesses beyond the creative industries). Nearly, all of the participants identified far more strongly as an artist or a creative person than as an entrepreneur. Many of the tensions, including a perception that the wider arts world was opposed to commercialisation of their (the participants') art work often left participants flailing, without the knowledge or confidence to behave entrepreneurially.

Conclusion

This article has provided insight into the lives of fine art graduates and the sometimes complex relationship they have with creativity, and how their training impacted on their careers and on their status as employees and as self-employed workers. What is clear is that this group strongly identified with being an artist and expressed a strong 'compulsion to create'. In amongst the stories provided by the participants are insight into how they continue to manage their compulsion to create and how this spills over into other sometimes non-artistic aspects of their careers, in terms of how they approach tasks, manage and motivate themselves.

The scale of this study means that, while rich and insightful, the findings are not generalisable, they do provide a starting point for further research. Future research could usefully look to a broader cohort to examine whether or not these findings are transferable and whether or not they are unique to fine artists. This would offer an opportunity for deeper exploration of the spillover effects of their creativity into the wider workplace and offer a better understanding of the contribution those trained in fine art make to the workplace. Amongst these findings are implications for educators within creative disciplines, and particularly fine art educators. What was evident was that teaching methods, or the art school pedagogy, reinforced artistic identity. This suggests that lecturing staff have a responsibility for managing the expectations of students, but also should recognise themselves as potential role models. While careers ranged from those embedded, specialists to non-creative, entrepreneurship continued to feature in terms of continued forays into self-employment. It was clear that while explicit enterprise education was limited if not non-existent within their fine art degree, it is important to consider its role. This is not about imposing a hard economic imperative on the world of fine art. It is about helping enable those artists to continue practising. This is an important distinction and suggests that the teaching of enterprise could be delivered by other fine artists or subject-specific experts, as opposed to generic enterprise educators.

The benefits of a fine art education to the wider workforce remain somewhat unexplored. Although for these participants, there is a suggestion that it provided them with an opportunity to truly explore their own ideas and philosophical positions. It offered them a freedom and a requirement to be self-managed that arguably provided them with lifelong skills. It also appears to have offered them the opportunity to approach their general working lives, regardless of destination, with a high level of creativity and problem-solving attributes. This suggests that there is scope to redress how we value fine art education and the potential contribution it makes.

It is important then, finally, to consider the careers of fine artists in terms of embedded creative work, in the broadest sense of the term. Of the participants discussed within this article, there is evidence that the nature of 'embeddedness' of a fine artist is harder to pin down. In the majority of cases, participants have what could be described as portfolio careers, generally made up of a core occupation within or outside the creative industries, in addition to their arts practice. There is a suggestion that, for the most part, they bring with creative expertise to the firms with whom they are employed; however, this does not manifest as clearly as it might for other creative disciplines. The creativity of the artists would seem not to be embedded in the same way as it might be, for example, for a designer. Instead, embedded artistic creative expertise often manifests as facilitation of others' creative output; this appears to be particularly the case of female participants and in the majority of cases in this study followed some further training. Although not the focus of this article, there are further indications that gender also has a bearing on the type of career and the balance and type of embeddedness of the career. For example, the female participants seem more likely to have an embedded facilitation role while simultaneously continuing their art practice, while male participants appear to be more traditionally embedded as creative roles, albeit not as fine artists.

While the participants' careers have evolved for the most part they started out hoping to forge careers as professional artists. They continue to aspire, albeit to differing extents, to work as artists. Career choices and trajectories have for the most part enabled participants to continue their arts practice or to satisfy their creativity.

References

Aggestam, M. 2008. "Art-Entrepreneurship in the Scandinavian Music Industry." In *Entrepreneurship in the Creative Industries: An International Perspective*, edited by C. Henry and A. de Bruin, 30–53. Cheltenham: Edward Elgar.

Ball, L., E. Pollard, and N. Stanley. 2010. *Creative Graduates Creative Futures*. London: Institute for Employment Studies.

Bilton, C. 2006. *Management and Creativity: From Creative Industries to Creative Management*. London: Blackwells.

Bridgstock, R. 2005. "Australian Artists, Starving and Well-nourished: What Can we Learn from the Prototypical Protean Career?" *Australian Journal of Career Development* 14 (3): 40–48.

Bridgstock, R. 2013. "Not a Dirty Word: Arts Entrepreneurship and Higher Education." *Arts and Humanities in Higher Education* 12 (2–3): 122–137.

Brooks, G. S., and J. C. Daniluk. 1998. "Creative Labors: The Lives and Careers of Women Artists." *The Career Development Quarterly* 46 (3): 246–261.

Carey, C. 2013. "Gender and Entrepreneurship in Creative Industry Career Journeys." PhD diss., Birmingham, AL: Birmingham City University.

Carey, C., and H. Matlay. 2007. "Entrepreneurs as Educators: The Case of the Creative Industries in the UK." *Industry and Higher Education* 21 (6): 435–443.

Carey, C., and H. Matlay. 2010. "Creative Disciplines Education: A Model for Assessing Ideas in Entrepreneurship Education?" *Education + Training* 52 (8/9): 694–709.

Carey, C., and A. Naudin. 2006. "Enterprise Curriculum for Creative Industries Students: An Exploration of Current Attitudes and Issues." *Education + Training* 8 (7): 518–531.

Henry, C., and A. de Bruin. 2008. *Entrepreneurship in the Creative Industries; An International Perspective*. Cheltenham: Edward Elgar.

Higgs, P., S. Cunningham, and H. Bakhshi. 2008. *Beyond the Creative Industries: Mapping the Creative Economy in the United Kingdom*. London: NESTA.

Howkins, J. 2001. *The Creative Economy*. London: Penguin Books.

Jones, S. 2011. *Changing Face of Artists' Employment a-n Research papers*. London: The Artists Information Company.

Kubacki, K., and R. Croft. 2011. "Markets, Music and All That Jazz." *European Journal of Marketing* 45 (5): 805–821.

Menger, P. M. 1999. "Artistic Labor Markets And Careers." *Annual Review of Sociology* 25: 541–574.

Oakley, K., B. Sperry, and A. Pratt. 2008. *The Art of Innovation: How Fine Arts Graduates Contribute to Innovation*. London: NESTA.

Penaluna, A., and K. Penaluna. 2009. "Assessing Creativity: Drawing from the Experience of the UK's Creative Design Educators." *Education + Training* 51 (8/9): 718–732.

Pratt, A. C. 2004. "The Cultural Economy: A Call for Spatialized 'Production of Culture' Perspectives." *International Journal of Cultural Studies* 7 (1): 117–128.

Throsby, D. 2007. "Preferred Work Patterns of Creative Artists." *Journal of Economics and Finance* 31 (3): 395–402.

The rise of the embedded designer in the creative industries

Katja Fleischmann and Ryan Daniel

School of Creative Arts, James Cook University, Townsville, Australia

Work practices in the creative industries have changed significantly since the turn of the twenty-first century. The design profession in particular has been influenced by rapidly emerging digital media practices and processes. While the design sector remains a significant source of employment, in recent years, there has been considerable growth in the number of designers working – or 'embedded' – in other sectors of the economy. The extent to which tertiary curricula cater for this shift in work practices and employment types is not well known. In this article, we report on original research on the preferred work destinations of a cohort of design students. This research was supplemented by a set of interviews with a small group of embedded designers in order to gain insights into the characteristics of embedded positions. Our research reveals that an embedded design position, while not well understood by undergraduate students, is a significant career path and one that should receive greater attention in undergraduate design curricula. We conclude that greater emphasis should be placed on assisting embedded designers to maintain creative networks that support them in what is a relatively isolated creative role.

The changing context of work and the creative industries

Over the past decade, the creative industries sector has been acknowledged as a key source of employment and contributor to economic growth in post-industrialised countries (Allen et al. 2013; Creative Industries Skills Council 2012). At the same time, economic developments, technological progress, globalisation and the global financial crisis have led to organisations across all sectors both 'slimming down and speeding up' (Bridgstock 2009, 33). Workers in general and in creative occupations in particular, therefore, need to be increasingly mobile, adaptable and able to adjust quickly to changing circumstances (Ball, Pollard, and Stanley 2010; Bridgstock 2009; Economist Intelligence Unit 2010; Haukka 2011). Key indicators of the changing work patterns of creative graduates include high levels of self-employment, a decrease in full-time employment, an increase in part-time, fixed-term or temporary work, multiple income streams and 'portfolio careers' (Bridgstock 2005; Ball, Pollard, and Stanley 2010, xxi; Comunian, Faggian, and Jewell 2011). Dynamic changes in the economy, in part as a result of the global financial crisis, have set an additional trend in motion with companies looking for creative people 'who could do two, three people's jobs' (Rann and Broderick 2010, 56); indeed, 'a tendency to do more with less is emerging' (McNamara 2010, 58).

Developments in digital technologies (for example, the Internet, mobile devices) and the emergence of new practices and services (for example, online games, online education) have contributed significantly to the growth of the creative industries and creative employment in other sectors of the economy (Department of Industry and Resources and Department of Culture and the Arts 2007; Skillset and Creative & Cultural Skills 2009). Consequently, new specialist professions, work processes and workplaces have emerged, all of which contribute to a move away from traditional career patterns. According to Harney (2010), the production of art has increasingly moved from studios or workshops into the workplace where artists use computers. The need for innovation in a highly competitive global economy has advanced digital technologies, particularly Web 2.0, to 'put co-creational processes on the centre stage', thus leading away from the individual as creator (Poettschacher 2010, 365). The United States Department of Labour estimates that '70% of jobs in 2020 do not exist today. This is because, based on the rate of development, the new technologies that define these new jobs have yet to be invented' (DesignSingapore Council 2009, 8). Reid, Albert, and Hopkins (2010, 7) agree with this assessment, arguing that there will be 'jobs and industries in 10 years' time that we have no conception of today. While new specialist professions will continue to emerge, existing ones may potentially evolve into embedded positions, where work practices normally outsourced to specialists are completed within the organisation. The Australian Research Council Centre of Excellence for Creative Industries and Innovation (CCI) proposes increasing growth in the number of embedded services:

> When a new activity emerges that requires a high degree of expertise or expensive specialist equipment it tends to be specialist firms that are established to provide the specialist services to the broader industry. As the technology becomes easier to use and cheaper it is more likely that these specialist occupations will become embedded in larger organisations who could have a frequent demand for the service. (Higgs 2005, n.p)

The creative industries sector with the highest number of embedded positions is design. In fact, designers are 'embedded in a wider range of other industries than any other sector'. For example, in Australia, designers and illustrators are employed in 129 different industries (Cunningham 2011, 31).

This employment phenomenon suggests that the education of designers is worthy of research attention, particularly given that design degree programmes have traditionally focussed on celebrity designers who gain near pop star status (Ashton 2009; Shaughnessy 2005). In fact, some authors argue that 'the promise of wealth and fame [is] deeply embedded in creative industry discourse' (Banks and Hesmondhalgh 2009, 418). This stands in contrast to recently emerging employment trends and changing career patterns. Further, in a major longitudinal study of the early career patterns of graduates in art, design, craft and media in the United Kingdom (UK), 48% of creative graduates felt that their course of study had not sufficiently prepared them for the world of work (Ball, Pollard, and Stanley 2010). This, therefore, raises the question of the extent to which design education adequately responds to contemporary employment issues and practices. How well is the career of an embedded designer understood by students? This article seeks to explore these issues.

Specialist and embedded designers

Globally, designers for print and interactive media design work mostly in small to medium size enterprises (SMEs). In the UK, for example, 60% of design companies employ fewer than five people and only 9% employ between 10 and 49 designers (Design Council 2010a). In Australia in 2008, only 1% of design companies employed more than 19 people (Department of State and Regional Development 2008). Designers are often self-employed, working freelance; this practice is also referred to as being a portfolio worker or having a portfolio career (Bridgstock 2005; Ball, Pollard, and Stanley 2010).

To a large extent, designers and their contributions have been invisible for a long time (Robertson 2004). However, this has changed in recent years through the work and research conducted by the UK's Design Council (ignited by the HM Treasury Cox Review 2005), along with the introduction of the Creative Trident methodology developed by the CCI (Higgs and Cunningham 2007; Higgs, Cunningham, and Pagan 2007). The Creative Trident methodology measures creative employment across the entire economy, not just occupations in the creative industries. Both embedded and specialist employment are measured (Higgs 2005; Higgs and Cunningham 2007). A 'specialist' is either self-employed or an employee of a creative enterprise, for example, a multimedia design studio, a graphic design or web agency, or a full-service creative advertising agency. An 'embedded creative' works outside the creative industries, for example, a designer employed in a pharmaceutical or manufacturing company to provide creative services 'in-house'.

In the UK, there are more designers working in embedded positions than there are in design consultancies. In a 2009 study, 82,500 worked in design consultancies while 83,600 worked in embedded roles (Design Council 2010a). Australia's creative industries workforce is similar, although it should be noted that the publicly available Census data aggregate architecture, design and visual arts. Of the approximately 118,000 people employed in these occupations in 2006, 49,508 were specialists and 42,892 in embedded positions (Higgs and Freebody 2008). In addition, a Census analysis of arts employment in Australia in 2006 (Higgs et al. 2010) reported specifically on graphic designers in arts-related occupations. Of this group, 300 worked in the arts industry, 15,570 were in broader creative industries, while 11,540 were in embedded positions (Higgs et al. 2010). Finally, a study conducted in Canada, exploring the career paths of designers in Toronto (Vinodrai 2006), revealed that of the 12,680 graphic designers in the city only 37.5% worked in the design industry. The others worked as designers in sectors, such as manufacturing, wholesale and retail. These findings, while not exhaustive in terms of the entire global design industry, certainly point to the significance of the embedded designer in the workforce.

Growth in embedded employment for designers

Embedded employment has certainly grown in the US, UK and Australia in recent years. In the UK, the number of designers working as part of in-house creative teams has increased by 8% since 2005 (Design Council 2010b). In Australia, embedded employment in the architecture, design and visual arts sector grew from 3.8% across 1996–2001 to 4.5% across 2001–2006, in contrast to specialist employment in this segment which declined from 4.4 to 3.3% during the same period (Higgs and Freebody 2008). Growth in embedded design employment is partially due to increased economic pressures. For example, 65% of companies in the UK that have expanded their in-house design departments cite cost effectiveness as a reason for doing so (Design Council 2010b). Another reason for this growth is the demand for design expertise in digital media (Department of Communications, Information Technology and the Arts 2006). Indeed, digital content creation (for example, for mobile devices) 'is the fastest growing sector in global media arts and is revolutionising the power and importance of creative industries in the 21st Century' (Department of Industry and Resources and Department of Culture and the Arts 2007, 3), a view recently supported by Goldsmith (2014).

Governments are increasingly recognising not only the social value of design but also its potential to contribute to economic growth (Design Council and Creative & Cultural Skills 2007; DesignSingapore Council 2009; HM Treasury Cox Review 2005; Woodham 2010). Over the last decade, design and designers have become key players in the business world (Commission of the European Communities 2009; Department of Innovation, Industry and Regional Development 2010; Design Council 2011) contributing to new areas including social design, service design, strategic design and design thinking (Design Commission 2013). Indeed, the embedded designer concept has been formalised by the Design Commission (2013, 31) as a 'full time strategic-level employee responsible for developing organisational design capacity, as well as for specific service redesign programmes'. Hence, there is significant likelihood that the embedded design sector will continue to grow, as industry, governments and organisations strive for efficiency, innovation and growth.

Graduate destinations: how undergraduate design students understand the world of work

Undergraduate design students are typically focussed on gaining employment in the creative industries upon graduation. Some may have had direct experience in the creative industries through casual, part-time work or through unpaid opportunities (for example, internships, work placements) prior to commencing their tertiary study. Others may obtain work while they are studying and thus learn about the nature of the creative industries. For example, a UK study conducted by Skills Online Group Limited (2011) found that 50% of graduates engaged in paid freelance work while they were studying. Design educators usually orient students towards professional practice by providing guest lectures, internships and work-oriented learning programmes, in order to equip design students with an understanding of the realities of the workplace, including the nature and types of careers in design (Fleischmann and Daniel 2010; Fleischmann 2012; Zelenko and Bridgstock 2014). Students' knowledge of industry practitioners' work practices, locations, career types and experiences may, therefore, exert an influence on the strategies they adopt in their transition from study to work (Clews 2009).

Tracking the destinations of design graduates is an emerging area of research, with recent studies offering some insights (e.g. Ball, Pollard, and Stanley 2010; Haukka 2011). One of the complicating issues is that most large studies aggregate various art and design disciplines; hence, it is not always clear how specific findings relate to designers. They at least offer some broad findings. For example, Ball, Pollard, and Stanley (2010, xxii) revealed that in the UK 'more than three quarters (78%) of working graduates were in creative occupations' up to 6 years after graduation. On the other hand, the Skills Online Group Limited (2011, 1) survey, also conducted in the UK, presented a different view of 2009/2010 art and design graduates, reporting that 'only 9.3% ... found a job in their chosen career [and] 51.3% had no option but to take a job outside of their field of study'. While these varied reports are no doubt influenced by the specific methodologies employed, the tracking of design graduates appears to be in an early phase, with more detailed and comparable studies needed in order to learn more about the career paths of design graduates.

One issue that emerges in some reports is that design graduates appear to lack realistic views of the job market and employment opportunities (Design Council 2005; Design Council and Creative & Cultural Skills 2007; Design Victoria 2009). According to the Sector Skills Councils for the Creative Industries in the UK, 'career paths across the sector are not necessarily well-known or understood by … graduates or their careers advisors' (Creative Skillset 2011, 37). In Australia, the largest creative industries student survey ever conducted (Haukka et al. 2009, 6) reported that around '70% of respondents … may have unrealistic expectations about their ability to find work in their preferred occupation given the outcomes for CI graduates'.

While the literature is substantial in terms of the need for a relationship between academia and industry, there is significantly less literature on how design students develop an understanding of the different types of careers in design, either within the creative industries or embedded in other sectors. If, or when, design students are given specific advice about career possibilities and work destinations and how students develop knowledge beyond what their educators share with them about the profession is unclear. It has been argued that there is a 'lack of differentiation made by colleges and universities between their courses and the possible career pathways for students' (Design Council and Creative & Cultural Skills 2007). The ways in which tertiary design programmes and schools currently provide career advice, including the preparation of design graduates for embedded positions, are (to a large extent) yet to be analysed in any depth. Therefore, the following two research questions emerge and are the focus of the remainder of this article:

(1) To what extent are undergraduate design students aware of and looking towards embedded positions once they have graduated?
(2) For those currently working as embedded designers, how did they attain this position and what are their views on this type of career path?

Methods and findings

Undergraduate design students at the School of Creative Arts at James Cook University, Australia, were surveyed over a period of 4 years (2009–2012), in order to explore students' aspirations about their future profession and workplace. Students were surveyed in the second year and again in the third year of their studies. A total of 197 students (102 second year, 95 third year) responded to the following online survey question: 'Where and in what occupation do you see yourself working after graduation?' Of the aforementioned cohorts from 2009 to 2012, three groups were also surveyed after graduation in 2009–2011, once they had been working for a year or longer. This was done in order to engage in follow-up research, including whether any were, in fact, working in embedded positions. Contact emails of these graduates were identified using various sources (for example, personal records of researchers, school database, Facebook, LinkedIn), with 88 contacts retrieved and graduates subsequently invited to participate in the online survey that explored position and type of employment held since graduation. Of those contacted, 34 participated (a response rate of 35.7%).

Figure 1 shows that design students envision working in a variety of commonly known careers in the creative industries. Students in third year are clearer about their preferences, with only 4% unsure compared to 19% of those in second year. It is also notable that new career options, such as video editor or motion graphic designer emerge in the third year, most likely a result of these areas of study being introduced during this time. Other career options disappear in the third year, most notably the special effects designer/animator and also the design educator. When analysing

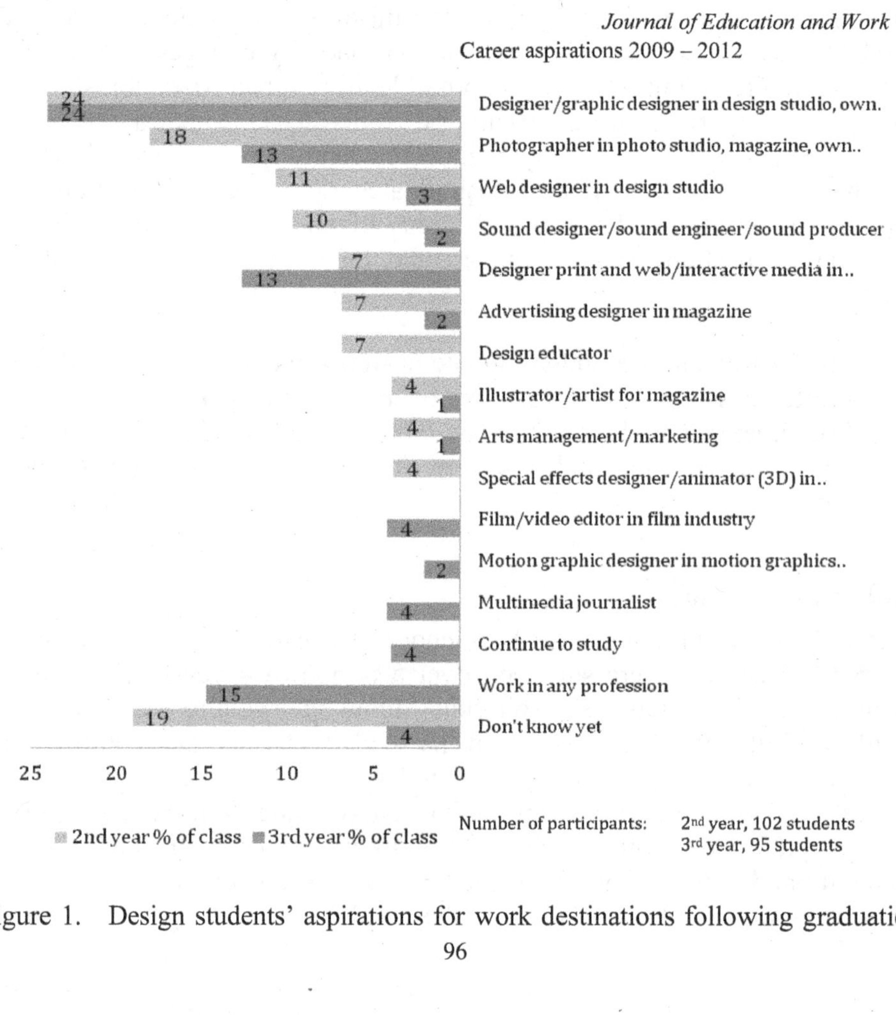

Figure 1. Design students' aspirations for work destinations following graduation.

comments and the kinds of companies referred to by the students, it is clear that the majority see themselves working in the creative industries. Only three students (all third year) made a reference to embedded employment; for example, one stated, 'I am going to be working for a local retailer doing web work and graphic design for print'. Overall, the data indicate that there are few explicit references to embedded positions, which suggests that, while employment in this area is significant, students seem to not be aware of it, or are not being exposed to and/or taught about it.

From the 34 graduates who had worked in the industry for one year or longer, 91% (31) had done so in a creative profession since leaving university. In terms of the total group, 50% (17) were employed by a company, 15% (5) were freelance, 15% (5) had their own business, 15% (5) had a combination of the aforementioned types of employment, while 5% (2) were not employed at the time of the survey. While the majority of graduates were working in the creative industries (68%), five were employed in embedded occupations in other sectors (15%). Table 1 provides an overview of the occupations graduates were working in at the time of the survey and the distribution across specialist and embedded positions.

While the majority of students did not envision embedded positions in their future (only 1.5% did), it is evident here that 15% (5) did in fact later

Table 1. Design graduates' occupation one or two years post graduation.

Current occupation of graduate	Number of graduates	%
Graphic designer	14	41
Graphic designer and photographer	4	12
Photographer	3	9
Web designer/interactive media designer	2	6
Producer	1	3
Graphic designer and illustrator	1	3
Arts administration trainee	1	3
Other non-creative industries occupations (e.g. sales assistant)	6	18
Not employed	2	6
Total	34	100
Position in the industry		
Creative occupation in creative industries (specialist)	23	68
Creative position in other sectors (embedded)	5	15
Non-creative occupation	4	12
Not employed	2	6
Total	34	100

obtain this type of position. This finding provides a starting point to explore the second research question, which endeavours to better understand how these students find their way into this form of employment.

In relation to the second research question, a sample of graduates working in embedded positions was contacted. While it would have been possible to deliver a survey to all design graduates, it was deemed more useful at this point to aim for depth and to, therefore, engage in interviews. Hence, the researchers initially aimed at finding out who was working in an embedded position. This was achieved by contacting recent graduates through email and Facebook, and seeking their advice and suggestions. Ten graduates were identified as potentially being employed in embedded positions. Of these, six responded to an invitation to participate in an interview, either face to face or over the phone if they were living in a different location. Prior to the interviews, the researchers developed a series of questions, in order to develop an understanding of the following:

- How and why they chose to undertake an embedded position.
- Details about the nature of their work as embedded designers.
- Their university study and knowledge of embedded positions.
- Future work issues.

The questions were drafted and subsequently re-drafted by the researchers, with the aim of looking at a range of influences and relevant factors. A copy of all interview questions can be found in Appendix 1. All six interviews were held over a two-week period and recorded for further analysis. While it would have been possible to create narratives about each particular position, upon analysis, it became clear that there were a number of commonalities across all of the designers' experiences. Hence, in order to provide an overarching picture of the issues, a table was used to summarise the responses to the questions. Table 2 provides the area of questioning in the first column followed by a summary of the response given by each of the six embedded designers (ED1, ED2, etc.).

There are a number of issues that emerge from the summarised responses presented in Table 2. One of the first is the fact that five of the six positions were either newly created (ED2, 3, 4), or grew from casual or part-time work into a full-time position (ED1, 5). Indeed, the rise of digital media systems and relevant marketing strategies is evident here, with several of the businesses recognising the need to venture into new areas of communication with customers. Another issue is that several interviewees referred to the particular challenges they had previously faced when attempting to secure work in design studios or agencies, such as the low level of pay, the intense competition for the work and the fact that employers were seeking experienced designers, not graduates. One designer, ED6,

Table 2. An overview of the six embedded designers' experiences and work profile.

Area of inquiry	ED 1	ED 2	ED 3	ED 4	ED 5	ED 6
Title of position	Product Manager	Project Design Officer	Graphic Designer & Photographer	Digital Marketing Coordinator	Marketing & Promotions Officer	Diary Manager
Company type	Science/laboratory microscopy provider	Regional council	Motor vehicle company	Residential construction company	Motor vehicle company	Political office
Time in position	7 years	1 year	2 years	13 months	3 months full time, casual work before	9 months
How position came about	Via family contact, commenced in casual position at university, became full-time shortly after	Applied for another position unsuccessfully but council created position based on skill set and portfolio	Applied for the advertised position	Applied for the advertised position	Working in non-creative position at same company; emerged over time as occasional creative jobs became full-time new position	Applied for the advertised position
Rationale for choosing an embedded position	Flowed on naturally given started there when studying, also didn't want to work in a design agency where told	Applied for numerous design positions but low paid and needing experience; current position much	Limited design agency jobs available at the time	I'd spent 12 months looking for design agency work; this position came up and I was offered it	Available design jobs were uninspiring or low level.	Wanted a position involving creativity but not the entire job; a balance of

(*Continued*)

Table 2. (*Continued*).

Area of inquiry	ED 1	ED 2	ED 3	ED 4	ED 5	ED 6
	what to do and work on	more pay and secure				organisation and creativity
Type(s) of work	Database management, web updates (capture, edit, load images), web coding updates, new website design	Rebranding of induction packages, refresh website, print and online media design, advertising design, posters, signage, invitations	Press advertising, web updates, e-marketing, signage (flags, banners, billboards), photography, administration	Brochure design, document creation, e-marketing (social media), print media, in-house style guides, promotional videos and show reels	Design for e-marketing, web updates, posters, internal: business cards, training booklets	Signage, flyers, event invitations, graphics for website, event and promotional photography
Skills, attributes required	Basic coding skills, product knowledge, knowledge of the business	Knowledge of creative suite, understanding of clients, writing and photography skills	Graphic design, photography, client relationship and administration skills	Software skills, camera skills, print processes, basic marketing knowledge, information design	Photoshop, illustrator, basic web knowledge, layout skills, ideas generation	Organisation, design software, photography and interpersonal skills
Taught about the position at university?	Not really; recalled a lecturer who had a similar position previously	It was covered in some design subjects	It was briefly covered from memory	Minimal, mostly focussed on design agencies or studios	Not really, more about designers as sole traders or freelance	Not really, couldn't recall direct learning

Embedded work at university?	Yes, had started in this position in first year on a casual basis	Yes, as a designer and photographer for a large mining company	No, just doing some administration in a hospital	No, mostly volunteer work in creative sectors	Volunteer work for community groups, police, others	No, did creative work for an architect
Place of internship while at university	Small photography studio	Photography and design studio	Photography studio	Video/photo studio	Fashion festival	Fashion designer
Advantages of the position	No time pressures or deadlines, flexibility in work days, relaxed, variety, travel to conferences	I have a very secure position, I'm the only designer	Opens up more job opportunities	Gave me a lot of confidence, learnt quickly, only creative person, variety	Own boss, creative freedom, colleagues accept creative options	Position is creative and interesting but includes organisation and planning
Disadvantages of the position	Limited career progression opportunities	Limited creative people around me, I rely on research for creative ideas	Creative work is outsourced if major administration tasks need to be done	Limited creative support and ideas, having to be self-motivated	No design colleagues to bounce ideas off	Time consuming job (long hours) so no creative work beyond position
Future in this position or type of position?	Yes, I hope to stay for 20 years. Long term future more likely to be in management	Definitely, I plan to stay and make my way up the business. I'd seek a similar position if I moved	No future in the current position due to ethical issues; definitely for future positions	Yes, when I am more experienced and older	Yes, very keen to continue and stay in a similar position if moving on	Yes, not only in the current position but in future would seek out a

(*Continued*)

Table 2. (*Continued*).

Area of inquiry	ED 1	ED 2	ED 3	ED 4	ED 5	ED 6
						similar position
Where/when should this type of position be taught?	Early in third year was a good time	First year is too early – would recommend third year when thinking about the future	More help should be provided about what sort of creative person and career each student wants	In early part of second year so they can better know where they do or don't wish to work	Industry lectures or examples are good. Early is good so they get time to think about different positions	As early as possible, so they know about the opportunities

in fact never sought full-time employment in a design studio or agency, perceiving the intense competition associated with these positions. It is also the case that ED2, ED3, ED4 and ED5 all initially sought a position at a design agency, which reflects the focus of their studies and learning within their undergraduate study. Ultimately, these four found their way into an embedded position, which is now their preferred type of work.

In terms of the positions themselves, what emerged was a range of design-oriented tasks that each was responsible for. Indeed, most did a variety of work on a daily basis, a factor that held great appeal:

> I don't know if I could go back to a design agency, although I'm sure it would be fine. I like the diversity of what I've got here; it's completely unpredictable. It's not like the client comes in with a brief, you do their business cards, do them a flyer, you go to the next one. It's just completely different every day. (ED5)

The interviewees identified other benefits associated with embedded positions, including the fact that they could open up other job opportunities in the broader employment sector (ED3), could be very secure and long-term positions (ED2) and could provide more creative licence and freedom (ED1, ED4, ED5). The latter benefit was summed up in the following comment: 'I'm basically sitting there in an office working individually. I'm my own person' (ED2).

Another emerging theme is what Bridgstock (2012) describes as the need for creative's to display 'enterprising' behaviours. Given that none of the interviewees had completed an internship as an embedded employee, the current position came about by promoting creative skills and potential contributions to an organisation or company. For example, ED2 had initially negotiated with a major mining company to undertake paid design and photographic work, then established a freelance creative business, and in the initial approach to the current employer ED2 made a point in mentioning the various creative skills developed through these prior experiences. Indeed, ED2's current position was created as a consequence of the interview and the employer's interest in ED2's creative skill set. Similarly, ED5 had previously undertaken various volunteer and freelance positions as designer and photographer. After obtaining an administrative position at a vehicle company, ED5 also made sure the managers knew about the variety of creative skills and ideas available to them. Over time, occasional creative jobs soon became so frequent that the company ceased outsourcing design work and created a full-time position.

While most felt that one of the main disadvantages of the position was the limited access to creative peers, all indicated a keen interest in either staying on in the current position or looking for further embedded positions. Most cited either the variety, job security, or higher levels of pay associated with embedded positions as the main reason for wishing to continue in their current or similar position. Furthermore, while indicating a long-term interest in moving into management, ED1 also vowed to continue to apply creative skills in the workplace, a statement supported by ED4, now working as an events coordinator for a large sporting organisation, who felt that design and other creative skills were a significant advantage not only when conceptualising events and ideas but also when discussing promotional strategies with both the marketing and in-house design teams. Indeed, the creative skills learnt at university can offer a competitive advantage, with ED6 stating that 'they employed me because I have a background in photography and graphic design – I think that got me over the line'.

Finally, each of the interviewees reflected on their studies and the extent to which they had been specifically taught about embedded positions and opportunities. Most were not readily able to recall specific detailed instruction and learning about the positions or, if they were, these were often informal experiences or brief references. Each then asserted the importance of informing students about these positions, most pointing to the second or third year after students have had an initial year in which to establish preferred areas of practice in design or other disciplines. Nevertheless, a relevant view was put forward by ED3, who felt that 'I don't think you can be totally prepared for the real world – every place [of work] is so different'. This reflection highlights the fact that, ultimately, design graduates will need to be flexible, motivated and committed if they are to establish a meaningful and viable career, an issue summed up by ED4: 'I relied on myself a lot. If I ran into a problem I had to turn to the Internet and manage multiple tasks. Somebody who isn't self-motivated could not do the job because there is minimal supervision'.

Discussion

While the authors readily acknowledge that this research reflects only a small sample of undergraduate design students and graduates from one institution, there is sufficient data to develop preliminary responses to both research questions. The majority of students surveyed in this research were not explicitly aiming for a career as an embedded designer, despite the fact that the literature reveals that approximately half of design graduates will work in this type of position (e.g. Higgs and Freebody 2008; Design Council 2010a; Cunningham 2011). The survey data support the claim that the embedded position does not currently receive sufficient attention within the undergraduate curriculum. Rather, the focus has been on preparing students to work as creative specialists. This tendency was also confirmed in the interviews. While this clearly points to the need for the current curriculum to be updated at the researchers' institution, it is reasonable to assume that other design schools might also need to pay additional attention to informing design students about embedded positions, considering that career opportunities are still not well understood across the creative industries (e.g. Haukka et al. 2009; Creative Skillset 2011).

The interviews revealed that designers work in embedded positions either as a consequence of applying directly for such a position or, alternatively, having the position created for them as employers become aware of their creative capacities and skills. Further, the rise of digital media in the workplace is evident, with two graduates moving into embedded design positions in order to enable the relevant company to develop a stronger brand and social media presence in the market. This finding aligns with the literature that cites the growth of digital media practices within industry (Department of Communications, Information Technology and the Arts 2006) and the potential for an increase in the number of embedded positions as new technologies become increasingly common within business (Higgs 2005). In fact, all of the designers interviewed were responsible for a number of marketing-oriented tasks including the design and development of creative artefacts. Overall, all six designers had a positive view of the embedded position and were keen to continue working in their current roles or in similar ones in future.

The interviews with embedded designers also reveal that the creative freedom attained by working alone in an organisation has both positive and negative aspects. While there is the advantage of having significant creative licence, it is also a challenge to not have regular access to creative peers and/or colleagues. This suggests that educational institutions could play a role in establishing and/or promoting professional networks of creative practitioners, including those working in embedded roles. Further, while enrolled in higher education, students should be given significant guidance about the specifics of embedded positions, as well as their employment characteristics and needs. Specifically, this might be achieved within undergraduate curricula through such activities as follows:

- direct instruction about embedded positions within the broader employment sector, as well as those specific to the creative industries and design;
- direct instruction about the use of social media in sustaining creative and other forms of professional networks;
- the involvement of embedded employees in industry panels and/or presentations to students;
- the placement of student interns with embedded practitioners, and
- the requirement that students research and investigate the types and locations of embedded positions within their specific sector of the industry, as well as the professional bodies that provide a source for networking and communication.

Conclusion

The design profession is changing, as is the contemporary workplace; it is increasingly showing an emphasis on exploiting those strategies and work practices that drive economic and public sector innovation. This trend is likely to continue, as more contemporary operations seek to establish a niche or capture new markets. Thus, the importance of embedded creative workers or teams is growing steadily. While the embedded design position ultimately offers advantages and disadvantages for graduates, it appears critical that contemporary educational institutions place greater emphasis on this type of employment. In addition, institutions should highlight the importance for any creative graduate to display enterprising skills, initiative and the ability to analyse and understand creative industries' employment patterns and opportunities.

References

Allen, K., J. Quinn, S. Hollingworth, and A. Rose. 2013. "Becoming Employable Students and 'Ideal' Creative Workers: Exclusion and Inequality in Higher Education Work Placements." *British Journal of Sociology of Education* 34 (3): 431–452.

Ashton, D. 2009. "Making it Professionally: Student Identity and Industry Professionals in Higher Education." *Journal of Education and Work* 22 (4): 283–300.

Ball, L., E. Pollard, and N. Stanley. 2010. Creative Graduates Creative Futures. Creative Graduates Creative Futures Higher Education Partnership and the Institute for Employment Studies. Accessed April 26, 2013. http://www.creativegraduates.com

Banks, M., and D. Hesmondhalgh. 2009. "Looking for Work in Creative Industries Policy." *International Journal of Cultural Policy* 15 (4): 415–430.

Bridgstock, R. 2005. "Australian Artists, Starving and Well-Nourished: What Can We Learn from the Prototypical Protean Career?" *Australian Journal of Career Development* 14 (3): 40–47.

Bridgstock, R. 2009. "The Graduate Attributes We've Overlooked: Enhancing Graduate Employability Through Career Management Skills." *Higher Education Research & Development* 28 (1): 31–44.

Bridgstock, R. 2012. "Not a Dirty Word: Arts Entrepreneurship and Higher Education." *Arts and Humanities in Higher Education* 12 (2–3): 122–137.

Clews, A. 2009. "Dialogues in Art and Design: Promoting and Sharing Excellence." Paper presented at the GLAD conference, York St John University, October 21–22. Accessed April 4, 2012. http://www.adm.heacademy.ac.uk/resources/publications/adm-hea-publications/dialogues-in-art-and-design

Commission of the European Communities 2009. *Design as a Driver of User-Centre Innovation*. Accessed October 12, 2010. http://ec.europa.eu/enterprise/news room/cf/_getdocument.cfm?doc_id=2784

Comunian, R., A. Faggian, and S. Jewell. 2011. "Winning and Losing in The Creative Industries: An Analysis of Creative Graduates' Career Opportunities Across Creative Disciplines." *Cultural Trends* 20 (3–4): 291–308.

Creative Industries Skills Council 2012. *Creative Industries Skills and Workforce Development Report: Constructing, Mining, Sharing and Growing Human Potential through the Creative Industries*. Brisbane: Queensland Government.

Creative Skillset 2011. *Sector Skills Assessment for the Creative Industries of the UK*. Accessed November 22, 2012. http://www.creativeskillset.org/uploads/pdf/asset_16295.pdf?4

Cunningham, S. 2011. "Developments in Measuring the "Creative" Workforce." *Cultural Trends* 20 (1): 25–40.

Department of Communications, Information Technology and the Arts 2006. *Unlocking the Potential: Summary*. Australian Government. Accessed October 11, 2007. http://www.dbcde.gov.au/__data/assets/pdf_file/0006/39813/DCIAA_summary.pdf

Department of Industry and Resources and Department of Culture and the Arts 2007. *Digital Media and Arts in Western Australia*. Western Australia. Accessed August 7, 2010. http://www.screenwest.com.au/download.cfm?DownloadFile=0E1230B3-1708-51 EB-A688353E4F29A658

Department of Innovation, Industry and Regional Development 2010. *Victorian Design Action Plan 2011–2015*. State Government of Victoria. Accessed April 23, 2011. http://www.dbi.vic.gov.au/

Department of State and Regional Development 2008. *NSW Creative Industry: Economic Fundamentals*. New South Wales. Accessed August 8, 2010. http://www.business.nsw.gov.au/ … /pub_081212_nsw_creative_econ_fund_innov.pdf

Design Commission. 2013. *Restarting Britain 2: Design and Public Services*. Design Commission. Accessed April 20, 2013. http://www.designcouncil.org.uk/documents/documents/ourwork/insight/governmentpercent20reports/dc_restart ing_britain_2_report.pdf

Design Council. 2005. *The Business of Design*. Accessed July 15, 2007. http://www.designcouncil.org.uk/publications/The-Business-of-Design/

Design Council. 2010a. *Design Industry Insights 2010*. Accessed August 3, 2010. http://www.designcouncil.org.uk/publications/industry-insights-2010/

Design Council. 2010b. *Design Industry Insights 2010 – Factsheet*. Design Council. Accessed August 3, 2010. http://www.designcouncil.org.uk/our-work/Insight/Research/Design-Industry-Research-2010/

Design Council. 2011. *Design for Innovation: Facts, Figures and Practical Plans for Growth*. Design Council. Accessed January 11, 2012. http://www.designcoun cil.org.uk/publications/Design-for-Innovation/

Design Council and Creative & Cultural Skills. 2007. *Design Blueprint*. Accessed September 11, 2008. http://www.designcouncil.org.uk/Documents/Documents/Publications/Design_Blueprint_Design_Council.pdf

Design Victoria. 2009. *Designing Our Future: A Report on Tertiary Design Education in Victoria*. Accessed January 15, 2010. http://www.business.vic.gov.au/industries/design/overview/designing-our-future

DesignSingapore Council. 2009. *Dsg-II: Strategic Blueprint of the DesignSingapore Initiative, 2009–2015*. Ministry of Information, Communications and the Arts. Accessed September 18, 2010. https://www.designsingapore.org/pdf/Dsg_II_Strategic_Blueprint.pdf

Economist Intelligence Unit. 2010. *Global Firms in 2020: The Next Decade of Change for Organisations and Workers*. Society for Human Resource Management (SHRM). Accessed April 20, 2013. www.managementthinking.eiu.com/global-firms-2020.html

Fleischmann, K. 2012. "Industry-driven Design Education: How Much Should Market/Industry Dictate Pedagogy?" In *agIdeas Research: Design for Business*. Vol. 1, edited by G. Muratovski, 76–95. Melbourne: agIdeas Press.

Fleischmann, K., and R. Daniel. 2010. "Enhancing Employability Through the Use of Real-life Scenarios in Digital Media Design Education." In *Preparing Graduates for the Professions Using Scenario-based Learning*, edited by E. Errington, 85–96. Mt Gravatt: PostPress.

Goldsmith, B., 2014. "Embedded Digital Creatives." In *Creative Work beyond the Creative Industries: Innovation, Employment, and Education*, edited by G. Hearn, B. Goldsmith, R. Bridgstock, and J. Rodgers, 128–144. Northampton, MA: Edward Elgar Publishing.

Harney, S. 2010. "Creative Industries Debate." *Cultural Studies* 24 (3): 431–444.

Haukka, S. 2011. "Education-To-Work Transitions of Aspiring Creatives." *Cultural Trends* 20 (1): 41–64.

Haukka, S., J. Brow, G. Hearn, and S. Cunningham. 2009. *60Sox Report Volume 1: From Education to Work in Australia's Digital Content Industries. The Opinions and Practices of Aspiring Creatives in the Creative Industries*. Brisbane, Queensland: Australian Research Council Institute for Creative Industries and Innovation. Accessed August 3, 2010. http://eprints.qut.edu.au/29795/

Higgs, P. 2005. "Specialist vs. Embedded Employment." *Creative Digital Industry National Mapping Project*. Accessed July 27, 2009. https://wiki.qut.edu.au/display/NMP/Specialist+vs+embedded+employment

Higgs, P., and S. Cunningham. 2007. *Australia's Creative Economy: Mapping Methodologies*. Brisbane, Queensland: Australian Research Council Centre of Excellence for Creative Industries and Innovation. Accessed September 23, 2010. http://eprints.qut.edu.au/archive/00006228/

Higgs, P., S. Cunningham, and J. Pagan. 2007. *Australia's Creative Economy: Definitions of the Segments and Sectors*. Brisbane, Queensland: Australian Research Council Centre of Excellence for Creative Industries and Innovation. Accessed September 23, 2010. http://eprints.qut.edu.au/archive/0008242/

Higgs, P., and S. Freebody. 2008. *Australia's Creative Economy Information Sheet: Detailed Sheets on Employment in the Creative Segments in 2006*, 1–12. Brisbane, Queensland: Australian Research Council Centre of Excellence for Creative Industries and Innovation. Accessed September 23, 2010.

Higgs, P., S. Freebody, P. Anderson, and S. Cunningham. 2010. *What's Your Other Job: A Census Analysis of Arts Employment in Australia*. Sydney: Australia Council for the Arts.

HM Treasury Cox Review. 2005. *Cox Review of Creativity in Business: Building on the UK's Strengths*. HM Treasury. Accessed March 23, 2007. http://www.hm-treasury.gov.uk/cox

McNamara, T. 2010. "Fighting Back." *Desktop* 263: 58–59.

Poettschacher, E. 2010. "The Rise of the Trojan Horses in the Creative Industries." *International Journal of Cultural Policy* 16 (3): 355–366.

Rann, K., and M. Broderick. 2010. "Please Consider." *Desktop* 263: 56–59.

Reid, B., A. Albert, and L. Hopkins. 2010. *A Creative Block? The Future of the UK Creative Industries*. The Work Foundation. Accessed November 22, 2012. http://www.theworkfoundation.com/assets/docs/publications/277_apercent20creativepercent20block.pdf

Robertson, D. 2004. *The Invisible Designer*. Design Institute of Australia. Accessed April 26, 2013. http://www.dia.org.au/index.cfm?article=108&id=102

Shaughnessy, A. 2005. *How to Be A Graphic Designer Without Losing Your Soul*. Princeton: Princeton Architectural Press.

Skillset and Creative & Cultural Skills. 2009. *e-Skills UK: Strategic Skills Assessment for the Digital Economy*. Accessed October 10, 2010. http://www.e-skills.com/research/research-publications/ssa-for-the-digital-economy/

Skills Online Group Limited. 2011. *Creative Industries Students Rebel: Creative Graduate Research Report*. Accessed April 26, 2013. http://www.skillsonlinegroup.com/uploads/docs/UKpercent20Creativepercent20Graduatepercent20Researchpercent20Report_Skillspercent20Onlinepercent20Group_final.pdf

Vinodrai, T. 2006. "Reproducing Toronto's Design Ecology: Career Paths, Intermediaries, and Local Labor Markets." *Economic Geography* 82 (3): 237–263.

Woodham, J. M. 2010. "Formulating National Design Policies in the United States: Recycling the 'Emperor's New Clothes'?" *Design Issues* 26 (2): 27–46.

Zelenko, O., and R. Bridgstock. 2014. "Developing Agency in the Creative Career: A Design-Based Framework for Work Integrated Learning." In *Creative Work beyond the Creative Industries: Innovation, Employment, and Education*, edited by G. Hearn, B. Goldsmith, R. Bridgstock, and J. Rodgers, 211–225. Northampton, MA: Edward Elgar Publishing.

Appendix 1. Embedded designer interview questions

(1) Firstly, can you describe how you became employed as an 'embedded designer'?
(2) Why did you choose to become an 'embedded designer' over working with other designers in a design agency for example?
(3) Can you describe the type of work that you do in the position and for the business where you are employed?
(4) What specific skills, attributes, or knowledge do you require in your current position?
(5) Looking back on your university studies, to what extent were you taught about 'embedded' positions like the one you are in now?
(6) Did you work in an 'embedded' position (e.g. freelance, part-time) while still at university?
(7) Where did you do your internship while at university?
(8) What do you believe are the advantages of being in an 'embedded' position?
(9) What do you believe are the disadvantages of being in an 'embedded' position?
(10) To what extent do you see a future for yourself in this current position or for this current employer?

(11) Would you seek out another 'embedded' position in the future? Why?
(12) Looking back at your time at university, when do you think career information about 'embedded' positions in the industry should be given to students? In what way should this be provided?

Index